QUILTS
TO
WEAR

QUILTS
TO
WEAR

VIRGINIA AVERY

BELL & HYMAN
LONDON

First published in Great Britain in 1982 by
BELL & HYMAN LIMITED
Denmark House
37-39 Queen Elizabeth Street
London SE1 2QB

Published in the United States of America by
Charles Scribner's Sons

British Library Cataloguing in Publication data

Avery, Virginia
   Quilts to wear.
    1. Quilting   2. Dressmaking
    I. Title
746.46   TT835

ISBN 0-7135 1350-0

Color sections printed in Japan.

Printed in the U.S.A.

*To everyone who pushed and pulled,
encouraged, pressured, supported, pestered,
praised, criticized, complained, and stuck with me
from hazy idea to printed word.*

Thanks to Judy Avery and Karen Hanley for their great illustrations. Thanks to Brad Stanton for much of the photography, and to the contributing fabric artists for the rest.

CONTENTS

Color plates 1–24 follow page 32; plates 25–47 follow page 64; plates 48–72 follow page 112.

Most of us professionally involved in quilting—teachers, lecturers, writers and publishers, shop owners, collectors, and so on—agree that quilting reappeared as a major force in America in the early 1970s.

Of course quilting never completely died out, but it certainly was in poor health. There were always quilters who either didn't know about their precarious position—or didn't care—and continued to make quilts as they always had. This alone says something for quiltmaking in general.

In 1971 the Whitney Museum of Art in New York City mounted a show of quilts as abstract art, and this exhibit, more than anything else, was the kiss that woke the sleeping princess. It propelled quilting into the world of big business. For the first time quilts were recognized publicly and officially as something more than bed coverings. The 1976 Bicentennial celebration of America's two-hundredth birthday also gave a push and a shove. In the wake of the festivities came a tidal wave of Bicentennial quilts, the first of which was the now-famous Hudson River quilt, designed and coordinated by Irene Preston Miller. This rush of quiltmaking was sponsored by towns and villages, historical societies, libraries, and other interested groups; indeed, the quilts were group projects and as such enabled many people to become active participants in an exciting celebration. Now quilting was more than a fad or a new pastime; it began to infiltrate the whole country. Clearly it was an activity, a skill, and a talent whose time had come again.

Books about quilting began to appear. Some were excellent and ought to be around for a long time. Others should never have seen the light of day, and they will fade from view. Quilting magazines and newsletters enjoy huge circulations and keep quilters all over the country informed about events. Many quilt shops have opened; many have closed. The good ones stock an amazing array of fabrics and an equally amazing array of quilting supplies; often they supply teachers and offer classes as well. Quilt clubs have been established in many areas, some clubs so large that they have divided and subdivided into smaller, more manageable groups. Manufacturers, antique dealers, publishers, museums, and galleries have all hopped on the bandwagon, eager to share in this bounty. Happily, there seems to be enough for everyone.

INTRODUCTION

The most amazing phenomenon of all this activity, in my mind, is the quilt symposium. The first one, the ice-breaker, was held in Ithaca, New York, in 1976, followed by a symposium in Toronto in May 1977. Since then symposiums or conventions have been held everywhere, or so it seems. They can be on local, regional, or national levels and can range in length from one to four days, but the format is always similar, differing only by degree or size: a quilt exhibit, usually invitational or juried; workshops and lectures; an area where supplies may be purchased; and ongoing demonstrations, informal gatherings, films and slide shows, a show-and-tell time, and a fashion show that usually follows the final banquet.

I've been fortunate to be invited to teach and lecture at many of these symposiums, and I am always amazed at the number of quilters—usually women—who show up; I know what planning and dogged determination lie behind each of their efforts to be there. First they have to work out the finances; paying for transportation, hotel, meals, and incidentals usually does not come out of petty cash. Women who work outside the home must arrange time off from office or shop, whether it is charged as vacation time or leave of absence. Women who are at home and responsible for husbands and children have to find a friendly mother who will pick up and deliver her young in her absence (with payment in kind at a future date). Mothers also must post reminders of schedules and appointments; and, in addition to all this, they leave refrigerators and freezers stocked with prepared meals and a list of instructions for heating and eating! I sometimes think of these quilters as indomitable ships churning steadily through unpredictable seas with a destination in mind if not in sight.

At the early symposiums I met women (and men) who had knocked themselves out to make a marvelous quilt for the exhibit. I also noticed that most of the quilters at these conventions wore clothes decorated with patchwork or appliqué and perhaps had something special saved up for the fashion show. Gradually the bed quilts grew smaller, and wall versions became very popular—in fact, they still are. I think wall quilts will maintain their popularity since there seems to be no diminishing of interest in this area. Rather, something more has been added. A quilting symposium is the barometer and weathervane; it records changes in the quilting weather, and right now the winds are blowing in the direction of quilted clothes.

In a way, this new trend was predictable. A quilt is not made in a weekend, or even a month. It takes time and effort, precision and dedication, and naturally, when you finish you want your friends to see it. We crave respect and recognition from our peers, and there is absolutely nothing as intoxicating as listening to words of praise about your-self—especially when these words are called out loud and clear for all to hear.

So when you do make a quilt and there isn't an exhibit nearby, you invite your friends over to have a look at your masterpiece. Usually, whether you live in a house or apartment, this means you'll have to clean. It also means you'll probably have to serve coffee and doughnuts if the viewing is in the morning, tea and cookies if it is an afternoon showing, and perhaps wine and cheese if friends come in the evening. This may be more than you bargained for, but it is also something you need not be concerned about if you direct your energies toward quilted clothes. You simply wear your handiwork and go wherever the action is—the supermarket, the shopping center, the bridge game, lunch or dinner, ballet or ball, church or synagogue. What you wear proclaims your talent more boldly than a billboard; you can explore unlimited varieties and combinations of fabrics, colors, and designs. You also add the dimension of motion to your work, for the body is your canvas. The quilted clothes you create can be timeless, enduring, without season or other restrictions. They are unique and individual, truly one of a kind.

Quilted clothes certainly are not new. They go back in history further than I can count. At first, like bed quilts, they were purely functional, it being easier to keep warm wearing several layers rather than one. In time, beauty joined function, and quilted clothes, exquisitely worked, have graced royal and ecclesiastical courts for centuries. Today such clothes are also owned and worn by socialites and wealthy women who are constantly in the public eye. Today, for the most part, quilted clothes are designed and made by well-known haute couture designers, names familiar to most of us. These designers constitute the major design force, but there is now a smaller design group whose top-quality work ranks with the best.

You and I belong to this smaller group, and it is for you, the quilters, stitchers, and home sewers, that I am writing this book. When we design, sew, and quilt our own clothes, we have the best of all creative worlds. We are inventive and experimental; we can embroider, embellish, piece, appliqué, tie-dye, batik, silk screen and hand paint fabrics or use them as they are. We work with texture and composition, balancing shape and form. Our clothes can be whimsical, elegant, sophisticated, classic, or outrageous, but they are always unique. We recognize the harmony between function and beauty; these clothes are the performing arts, subject to no dictates other than individual taste and subject to no restrictions except those we impose on ourselves.

Quilters need just a basic knowledge of sewing and a friendly relationship with their sewing machine. If you can stitch quilt blocks, sashings, and borders in a straight line, you most certainly can stitch straight garment seams. Home sewers need only a basic knowledge of quilting to make their first quilted garments. Experienced quilters and home sewers can dive right in. It is certainly a talent and a skill to turn out a beautifully made garment, but that same garment with quilting added assumes a texture and dimension unattainable by any other method. Perhaps this texture, this effect, partly explains the hold quilting has over people, women especially. I am in awe of it. Not only is it creative and rewarding, but its soothing, healing mystique inspires a feeling close to reverence. It is an obsession—and understandably so. It seems to fill a hunger almost spiritual in intensity; it offers solace, renewal, and unadulterated joy. We no longer try to explain it but simply accept it as a treasured gift. Quilting, coupled with the creative satisfaction of creating your own wonderful clothes, is unbeatable.

I've met many of you who are now reading this book. You've been in my workshops, heard me lecture, been in fashion shows I've commentated. You've read many of the articles I've written and *The Big Book of Appliqué* and used it to help you in your work. *Quilts to Wear* can help you too. It isn't a pattern book. The stores are filled with patterns ready to buy; there are graphed patterns and diagrams in other books for you to enlarge and use; and magazines often have patterns as well. This book won't teach you how to quilt or sew, but it will help you to combine the best of both the quilting and the sewing worlds. With it you can develop a design, choose fabrics and combine colors. It will help you to polish your hand- and machine-quilting skills. Machine quilting is an area almost untouched as far as bed and wall quilts are concerned, but it offers new and exciting effects when used in quilted garments.

Of course you have to do your part. You have to be receptive and open, eager to experiment, and willing to make mistakes, for that is how we all learn. Everything we do, whether it's called art or craft, is based on tradition, as are our lives. Everything evolves from what has gone before, but what makes our work fresh, invigorating, and fulfilling is our ability to use tradition in a new context, crossing over and bending old established lines. So on with it; the opportunity is yours.

TO HAVE ON HAND

The right tools, the proper equipment, makes any task easier. I know a few people (a very few), both quilters and home sewers, who thrive on adversity and deprivation and consider it a challenge to turn out something smashing against all odds. It's a challenge all right, but I don't like to work that way, so over the years I've collected a lot of Virginia-helpers, staunch and dependable friends. Here are some of them.

HAND-SEWING NEEDLES

You can use sharps, betweens, or quilting needles. Have an assortment on hand, sizes 7 to 12. I find I use quilting needles for all types of hand sewing now—basting, piecing, appliqué, and quilting. They are short and sharp, and I am used to them. I usually use an 8, sometimes a 10. I have so much difficulty threading the 12s that I don't use them very often, but I keep them on hand because I think it makes a good impression. Use crewel needles for embroidery flosses and heavier threads; they have large eyes to accommodate different sizes of yarn and floss. You should have a few tapestry needles; these have large eyes and blunt ends, and you'll need them for trapunto cording. Sizes 16, 18, and 20 will give you an adequate assortment.

MACHINE NEEDLES

These are as important as hand-sewing needles. For a domestic machine you should have 11s, 14s, and 16s and, for an imported one, 70s, 80s, 90s, and 100s. There are special wedge-shaped needles for sewing leather or suede, although it is seldom necessary to use them; most of the time a regular needle works quite well. You should also have double and triple needles for decorative stitching and quilting; these are usually mounted on a single shank, and you can find them at your sewing machine dealer. If you plan to do any stitching on knits, you should have some ball-point needles.

THREADS

There are cotton, polyester, and cotton-covered polyester threads on the market. I find that many of the American-made threads are of poor quality, but Coats and Clark and American Thread are the best of these. Other threads fray, ravel, and tangle, particularly in hand sewing. They also tangle my disposition. I think they work better on the machine, but most of the time I use imported threads, which are excellent. Gutermann, Molnlycke, and Mettler are the three best-known brands in the United States, and they are now available in most shops. In the United Kingdom, Sylko 50, a cotton thread, and Gutermann and Drima, both polyester threads, are the most suitable. I use them for both hand and machine sewing, and they can be used for both sewing and quilting, although there are special quilting threads on the market. Most quilting threads are good, even the American-made ones, heavier than regular thread, strong, and lightly coated with silicone. You could also use a heavy-duty sewing thread for quilting. Two silk threads, size A for regular sewing and quilting, and a silk buttonhole twist are good to have on hand. The twist can be used in embroidery or quilting, either by hand or by machine. Metallic threads come in gold, silver, and bronze shades, and they are effective for decorative stitching. Nylon transparent thread has a place in your thread box too. I use it occasionally for machine work, but then only in the needle assembly; it is too springy to use in the bobbin. Another thread, made by D.M.C. for machine embroidery comes in solid or variegated shades and works very well.

YARNS AND FLOSSES

You should have a good assortment of yarns and flosses, ranging from fine baby yarns to tapestry yarn, six-strand embroidery floss, and a selection of perle cotton. Nubby, thick, uneven yarns can be used for hand or for machine couching.

BEESWAX

Tuck a little wheel of beeswax in your thread box. When you thread your needle for hand sewing, run the thread through one of the slots in the plastic wheel. A light coating of beeswax usually will make any rebellious thread snap to attention.

PINS

You need sharp, rust-proof pins. I recommend two types. Iris pins are long, thin, and sharp, and they come in a round blue metal box. Japanese pins are also long and sharp and have little pastel flower heads. (In the United Kingdom choose lace or bridal pins. The smaller Lillikins are useful for finer work.) Cheap, inferior pins will rust in your fabric and filler or batt if left longer than a few hours. Beware!

THIMBLES

Primarily you need a thimble to fit the middle finger of your sewing hand. Use either the end or a side of it to push the needle through the fabric; it is an absolute must in hand quilting, and it may save you from bleeding to death, or worse, from getting blood stains all over your quilted garment. (Your own saliva is the most effective way of removing a fresh bloodstain.) When you are hand quilting it is a good idea to keep a thimble on the index finger of your other hand—the one you keep underneath while you're quilting. Wearing one there might save you from going through life with a permanently perforated finger.

CUTTING TOOLS

Neither toenail nor cuticle scissors have a place in your sewing box. Buy the very best scissors and shears you can afford; it is an investment. Don't let anyone else use them, especially your family. Buy some for them and consider this an investment too; it just may keep them away from yours. You need very sharp shears for fabric; I think Ginghers are probably the best. They are very sharp and will cut accurately through several layers of fabric. You also need small scissors for trimming and clipping. When you go scissors shopping, take a little bag of scraps with you and try cutting various weights and layers; the shears and scissors you are considering as a purchase should have very sharp blades and cut cleanly to the point.

Pinking shears are nice to add to your sewing box, but they are used only as a decorative aid after a seam is stitched.

The Olfa rotary cutter is an excellent cutting tool, especially for strip or string piecing. With it you can cut several layers of fabric accurately at the same time, so it is a great timesaver. The cutter comes with its own self-sealing cutting surface, which saves you from carving deep grooves in the dining room table. The cutter also comes with extra blades, if you remember to order them, and you should.

Another good cutting tool for strip work is an eighteen-inch (46 cm) paper cutter, available at most stationery or office supply shops. You also should have scissors for cutting paper, cardboard, and plastic, and perhaps a pair of the little "thumb clippers" for clipping threads.

MEASURING TOOLS

You should have a see-through ruler and yardstick, a T-square, and a flexible tape measure. An architect's triangle and a French curve are also handy, and so is a protractor. All of these are available in either inches or metric measure. A compass is essential for design work. You can get a little six-inch-radius compass at any stationery store, but you will get far more use and satisfaction if you buy a compass with extensions at an art supply store. Anthony di Chesere of Victory Tool and Die Company has developed a clear plastic ruler that can easily be used as a compass with the aid of two sharp pencils. One ruler will give you up to a twelve-inch (30 cm) radius, a second up to twenty-four (60 cm). You can always substitute by tying a string around a pencil, but this method is inaccurate and unsatisfactory.

Victory Tool and Die also carries a complete line of metal templates for use in piecing and quilting. They are available at most quilt supply shops as well as in the vendor areas of the symposiums. (See page 138 for a list of suppliers in the United Kingdom.)

A Fashion Ruler from Fashionetics will help you if you have any tricky changes in a paper pattern before you cut into fabric.

GLUE STICK

Useful while you are developing patterns on paper, a glue stick is also very helpful in appliqué work and some other stitching. It holds two layers of fabric together and makes it easier to sew them. Spray starch sometimes will serve the same purpose.

MASKING TAPE

Use masking tape to hold patterns, paper or fabric, together temporarily; it is easier to use than Scotch tape and easy to remove from fabric when you are finished. Masking tape in various widths is invaluable to a quilter; use it to mark straight quilting lines.

MARKING TOOLS

These are very important. I've seen many an otherwise fine piece of work spoiled by the residue of marking—most often in soft pencil—which simply will not come out. You should avoid these at all costs. Use soft lead pencils only for writing; otherwise use no. 3 or no. 4 hard lead pencils (2H in the U.K.). You need white or pastel marking pencils for dark fabrics; Col-erase or Caran d'ache pencils work well. Chalk pencils work too, but do not use tailor's chalk; it has too much wax in it and is difficult to remove. I'm also partial to soap slivers for marking. In stitching a garment, notches are used for joining sections together with accuracy; tailor tacks can be used in the fabric as well. I do not use dressmaker's carbon or the little dressmaker's wheels; I think the cutting edges of the wheel damage the fabric, and I also think they make it almost impossible to transfer accurate marking.

OTHER SUPPLIES

You will need tissue and tracing paper, pattern paper, graph paper, a notebook, and pen or pencil. You also need a good steam iron, a press mitt, transparent press cloths, and an ironing board or other suitable ironing surface.

SEWING MACHINE

A good sewing machine is essential. I consider it as important and invaluable as my bed, my piano, or my stove. The machine does not need to be one of those fancy, sophisticated types with a built-in computer that does everything but talk back to you, but it should be in good working order—clean, oiled, and with tensions and stitches balanced and regulated. If it has a built-in zigzag, fine; if not, those attachments can be purchased. You should have the instruction book for the machine too, and refer to it frequently. You will find, hidden on many of its pages, little nuggets of information that will prove invaluable if you take the time to read them and try them out. The sewing machine is a marvelous friend, and too often it has been maligned and misunderstood. I often wish I had invented it.

I'll talk about patterns, fabric, and fillers later on, but before I end this chapter I want to remind you that you also need time and space for your work. Often it is a matter of rearranging or rethinking your priorities, of realizing that what you do and when is of major importance. We attach a false importance to chores; we procrastinate without realizing it; we permit family and friends to usurp time that belongs to us, and we must reclaim that time. This undoubtedly will involve choices, but we all make them. You may have to juggle spousing, entertaining, and parenting in order to claim your time. You may have to forego regular house cleaning and laundry (I consider this no sacrifice, just clever planning). If you work full or part time at another job in another field, you may need another set of criteria for juggling evening and weekend time. I leave the details to you.

Working space is as important as working time. Hallelujah to those of you who have a guest room or similar area that you can convert for your own use. Those of you who are already dedicated and serious workers may have a studio or workroom that is off limits to everyone but you except by special invitation. Failing this, plan a quiet but aggressive takeover of the TV room, den, dining room, or half the kitchen. Start small, perhaps in a corner, then gradually fill the rest of the space. In a remarkably short time, your work space will be a *fait accompli*, leaving a bewildered family in the wake. When you have finally established your beachhead, don't give an inch. Keep your defenses in order at all costs.

2

PATTERNS: PITFALLS, AND POSSIBILITIES

In the Introduction I explained that this is not a pattern book; I could never compete, nor do I wish to try, with patterns so readily available to you. You can make a selection from the big counter books in the fabric store or choose from a scaled or graphed pattern in a book or magazine. You will have to enlarge the latter, but if you like the style of the garment, and if you plan to use it more than once, it is worth the effort. Most basic pattern designs can be varied any number of ways.

Our life styles, along with everything else, have changed drastically in the past few years. Fashion and the rules of fashion—if there are any—have changed too. Boundary lines have been breached or have vanished altogether. Few of us have need for true formal wear; the evening dress or ball gown is an anachronism. What goes to the office can also go on to dinner later. Our skirts, dresses, and pants can be any length and style and still be acceptable. Our outerwear runs the gamut from simple quilted jacket to elaborate coat, enveloping shawl, cape, or poncho. This is an era of seasonless dressing, and we need only reconcile fabric and filler to accommodate such dressing.

It's also a mix-and-match world. A jacket or vest can be worn interchangeably with a dress, a skirt and blouse, or slacks and sweater. We can pile layer on layer to get us through the deep freeze, both indoors and out, for in these energy-conscious times our houses are cooler than they used to be. And in the hotter-than-you-know-what times we can remove unneeded layers. No matter what the climate though, quilted clothes can add to warmth and aesthetics.

Patterns for quilted clothes should be simple. You lose much of quilting's effect if you stitch up a pattern with a great many seams. Many commercial patterns that can be adapted for quilted clothes have unnecessary seams, and such seams can often be eliminated by combining two pattern sections, matching seam line to seam line. This does not affect the appearance of the garment, especially if the seams are straight ones. In fact, they add appreciably to the final quilting design.

The design and color of your garment—plus the quilting, of course—are the stars in the show, and they will give any simple pattern a special aura. Many of today's patterns are based on ethnic clothes, and with good reason. Ethnic styles come from Mexico, Central and South America, the Far and Middle East, Africa and Asia, and Central and Eastern Europe, in fact, from everywhere. The fabric lengths are governed by the width of the looms, and these ethnic garments, though different in color, weave, and ornamentation, are designed to be joined together in panel width. Usually the fabric is not cut at all. These clothes are known for comfort and ease in wearing; they are timeless and are often passed on from generation to generation.

In most of the countries mentioned, both men and women learn to weave when they are children. Native villagers' clothes are made from loom lengths, rarely cut into and sewed from selvedge to selvedge. These clothes, too, are based on simple geometric shapes—the square, the rectangle, the triangle.

Many of us have adapted these patterns and designs for our own use, and pattern companies, their fingers always on the pulse of the home sewer, have produced many patterns based on these same styles. The Folkwear Pattern Company, based in California and a relative newcomer to the commercial pattern world, has established itself solidly in its offerings of ethnic patterns, offering selections from Af-

1. *Quilted jacket in progress, by Lesly-Claire Greenberg. Notice that the square-cut design is ready to have the sleeves joined; after this, side seams will be sewed and outside edges finished.*

ghanistan, Bolivia, Tibet, Turkey, China, Japan, and other countries, each pattern based on an authentic dress but readily adaptable to individual design. These patterns are printed on substantial stock, with cutting and sewing lines marked for three different sizes, a standard seam allowance of one-half inch (12 mm), and adequate directions and diagrams. I have used a number of these patterns, particularly the Turkish coat and the Tibetan sleeveless coat, changing fabric, color, and detail each time. Both of these patterns are based on fabric sections or panels that are seamed together, but you can eliminate some of these seams if you are working with a wider fabric. I think these patterns run a little large, but they are easy enough to cut down for a proper fit.

Yvonne Porcella has developed her own ethnic patterns in several small books; her *Pieced Clothing* has fourteen patterns for outerwear, most of them quilted. These are not full-sized patterns, of course, but specific diagrams and measurements that enable you to cut directly into your fabric and eliminate a paper pattern. If you plan to use a pattern or design more than once, you might want to cut the pattern from paper, Trace-a-pattern, or muslin.

Maggie Lane in *Oriental Patchwork* offers scaled pat-

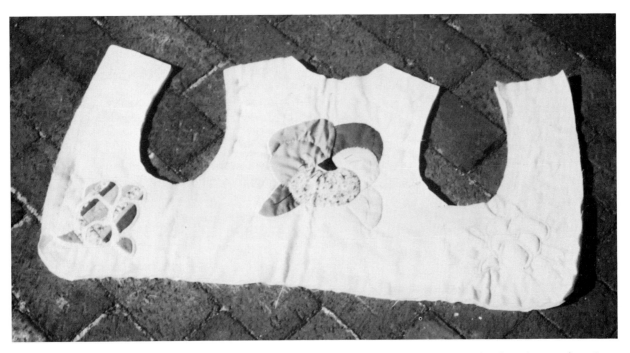

2. *Another garment in the making. This quilted vest by Kathy Mauser for her daughter is hand appliquéd and hand quilted. (The photo was taken in a Nantucket seminar taught by the author.)*

Fig. 1a. *Jacket with set-in sleeve.*

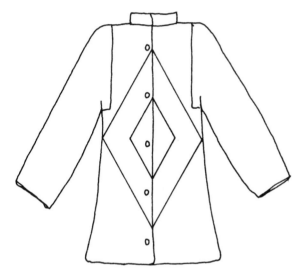

Fig. 1b. *Jacket with square-cut sleeve.*

Fig. 1c. *Jacket with raglan sleeve.*

terns that must be enlarged to size. These are simple, easy designs suitable for our relaxed society.

The Big Four pattern companies—Vogue, Butterick, McCall's, and Simplicity—have recognized the validity of quilted clothes in the past few years. They offer many patterns specifically for quilting, but many others not so designed can be quilted with great success. I'm not going to give you any of the pattern numbers because by the time you have this book the patterns will be obsolete. All the "commercial" companies do this, as I suppose they must to stay in business, turnover being the big thing. Pattern sales are regularly reviewed, and if certain patterns don't meet their quota they are "pulled," that is, dropped from circulation. Occasionally a very popular pattern will be pulled, and I'm suspicious when that happens, for very often it will reappear at a later date with few changes but at a higher price. Well, we all have to make a living, and the Big Four are geared to constant change in fashion.

Usually several patterns are offered each season for quilted clothes; the quilting designs are simple and unimaginative, for the most part straight-line or channel quilting. These patterns are, of course, designed for a mass market, so the individual sewer and quilter must be responsible for changes. But, as I mentioned, you need not limit yourself to quilted-garment patterns; you can quilt any style of garment whether the pattern description says so or not. Folkwear patterns do not change; they go on year after year, and availability is no problem. As for Big Four patterns, however, when I see a pattern I like or one I might use in the future, I buy it. True, I have some patterns now that have never been opened and may never be, but I've also had some disappointments over patterns I wish I had bought when I had the chance.

Try to select a simple pattern, no matter what type of quilted garment you want to make. Remember, you may be piecing, appliquéing, or quilting the garment with designs you've developed, and you don't want to clutter it with unnecessary seams or construction lines. Although I am emphasizing outerwear in this book, all of the information or directions may be applied to any type of garment—skirts, pants, dresses, and more.

The following sections give some pattern guidelines.

SLEEVES

A set-in sleeve has a shaped cap, or top, that is eased into the armseye at shoulder and underarm areas. The cap can be smooth, as in classic styles, or pleated, puffed, or gathered at the seam line. Too many gathers in a quilted sleeve may cause excessive bulk.

A raglan sleeve can be either one- or two-piece. A one-piece raglan has a dart that runs from neck to shoulder to give a smooth fit. A two-piece raglan has a seam from neck to wrist; the fit, or dart control, lies in the shaping of the seam. If you lay the two sleeve pieces flat on your work table, you will see the sharp curve from shoulder to neck.

A kimono-style sleeve is cut in one with the body of the garment. There is usually a seam from neck to wrist but no armseye; this seam, joining front and back body sections, is cut on the bias grain of the fabric. The underarm section of this sleeve can start at the waistline (a dolman sleeve) or from any point higher up. If you cut it high near the arm, you may need to insert a gusset for ease in wearing. For quilted garments it is easier and better to cut the sleeve section so that this gusset is not necessary.

Rather than a shaped seam from neck to wrist, some kimono-style garments are cut straight across the shoulder. This is a true ethnic cut or style, and if you do use it you can often eliminate a seam at the shoulder line. Such sleeves are similar in style to the Japanese or Chinese kimonos, but the sleeve section is cut separately and added to the body of the garment. This is also the basis for the dropped-shoulder sleeve. The body of the garment is cut in one with the sleeve but does not go all the way to the wrist; the sleeve or dropped-shoulder section usually stops above the elbow, and a rectangular sleeve section is added for length. There are many variations on this loose, easy fitting sleeve; study them, or test one or two of them out, and decide which is best for you.

BODY STYLES

The simplest body style is straight, without darts, and cut in one piece from shoulder to hem. If you need a dart for fitting purposes on a straight garment, by all means use one; your clothes will fit better and look better. Mark dart stitching lines with visible basting, and do not quilt that area in order to eliminate bulk when the dart is sewed. If you plan a specific quilting design for this area, pin the dart together so that you can see how the design will look when the dart is sewed. Quilt only up to the stitching lines, with sections flat, and when the dart is sewed the quilting design will be unified and continuous.

Some pattern styles, rather than hanging straight, are fitted with construction seams. The most popular is the princess line, a seam that divides the front section of a garment

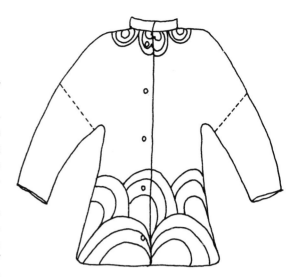

Fig. 1d. *Jacket with dropped shoulder sleeve.*

Fig. 1e. *Jacket with kimono sleeve, cut-in-one with garment.*

Fig. 1f. *Jacket with kimono sleeve with yoke.*

lengthwise from shoulder to waist or hem. A curved seam with built-in dart control, it holds the garment close to the body, curving outward over the bust, in toward the waist, and then out again over the hips. If nature has endowed you generously, you might be better off with a fitted pattern rather than a straight style with darts. Each front section can be quilted separately and then seamed together.

Either a fitted or straight-style pattern may have a yoke, either cut straight across front and back or curved or pointed from armseye to center front and back. Often such yokes can be quilted and the rest of the garment left unquilted. Dress tops and shirts fall in this category, and often vests and jackets do too, especially if a heavier fabric is used in the body of the garment.

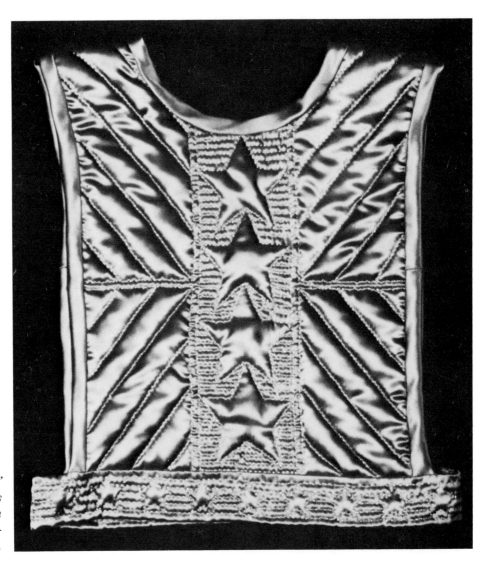

3. *"Star-Spangled Vest" by Colleen Craven. This vest was hand quilted on rust satin with gold metallic thread.*

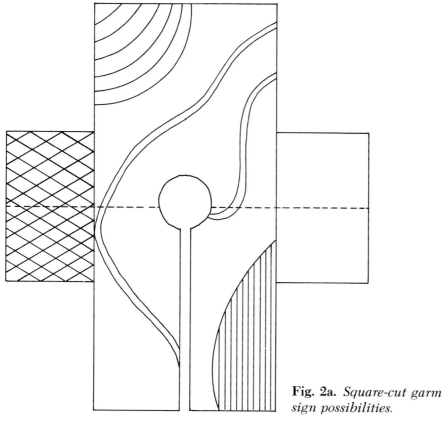

Fig. 2a. *Square-cut garment showing design possibilities.*

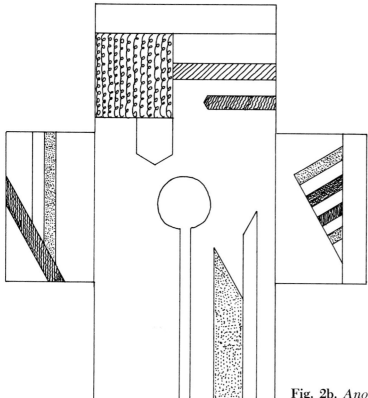

Fig. 2b. *Another version of a square-cut garment.*

NECK AND COLLAR STYLES

A plain collarless neckline is perhaps the easiest to do, but frequently it is not the most becoming. The neckline can be round, square, or V-shaped, and a scarf of the same or a contrasting material can be added to fill in.

A mandarin or stand-up collar is the easiest to make and is flattering to almost everyone. It is easy to sew and may be cut on a straight or bias grain. A straight-grain collar will stand up better, but a bias collar drapes better.

A shawl collar is cut in one with the front of the garment, and an under-collar section, cut on the bias, is added around the neck edge. A facing section, with one center back seam at the neck, completes the collar. This collar then folds back against the front of the garment and gives a continuous rolled look around the neckline; it is flattering, easy to construct and wear, and an easy style to quilt. Any commercial pattern or good sewing instruction book has diagrams and details telling you exactly how to do all these steps, although I imagine most of you already know how.

Remember the possibilities for change in any pattern. A garment that meets or closes at center front may easily be changed to a side or asymmetrical closing; decorative frogs or ties may be substituted for buttons.

CAPES AND PONCHOS

There are wonderful quilting possibilities with capes and ponchos. They are dramatic and are sometimes called "flings" or "sweeps," names that fit them very well when you think of their swashbuckling look. They are cut so that the fabric falls freely and covers the arm to the wrist; if the garment is longer, there may be slits or holes for the arm for ease in movement. A cape can be circular—in fact, a half-circle cape is easy to construct and to quilt and just as easy to wear. Or it can be fitted and closer to the body, in which case it has shaped seams from the neck over the shoulder and along the top of the arm, similar in fact to the seam of the kimono-style garment with the cut-in-one sleeve. The difference is, of course, that the cape doesn't have sleeves; the fabric is simply left uncut to flare around the hemline. Some cape patterns may be cut differently, but keep in mind that when you quilt your cape you want as few seams as possible.

Ponchos are similar to capes but are usually square or rectangular, often do not have a closing, and are made to

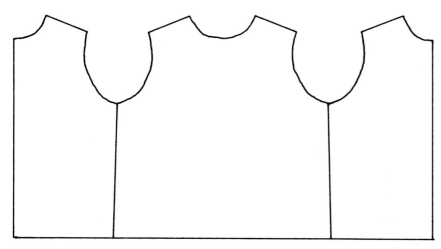

Fig. 3a. *Basic pattern pieces joined at side seams to facilitate design; the vest or jacket can now be cut without side seams.*

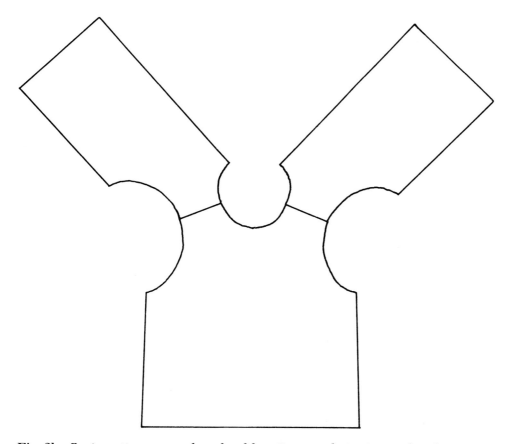

Fig. 3b. *Basic pattern seamed at shoulders for easy designing and quilting.*

4a. *Quilted butterfly jacket by Julie Draska. Made from a soft, velourlike fabric, the jacket is lined with a brown cotton print. (A Helen Richards pattern.)*

pull over the head. It is a simple matter to add a front closing if you want to, however. A poncho is perhaps the easiest garment to make without a pattern. Simply have someone measure you from wrist to wrist across the back of your neck, arms outstretched. This measurement is the width of your poncho and gives you the dimension of the square of fabric. If your fabric doesn't come this wide, add a length with a seam, or use strip patchwork or borders to gain the necessary width. Cut the hole for your head and neck opening in the center of this square. If the opening is cut on the straight grain, the poncho will fall straight, or horizontally. If you cut it on the diagonal, or bias, the poncho will fall in points at center front and center back and over the wrists. Face the back or bind off the neck opening, and add a collar if you like.

The same poncho measurement may be used for a half-circle cape; just round off the bottom edge instead of leaving it straight. The wrist-to-wrist measurement is the diameter of the half-circle, and these straight edges meet in front; cut the opening for the neck at the midpoint on the half-circle.

4b. *Detail of Julie Draska's jacket. The lotus pod, a Japanese symbol of fertility, has been used for the quilting design.*

DRESSES AND BLOUSES

A quilted dress or blouse can be beautiful, and being quilted doesn't mean it will be too warm. A lightweight fabric with thin or no filler works beautifully in this case. This approach also works with skirts and pants. Unless you are thin, try to stay away from bulk at the waistline; choose a pattern that has a smooth fit across tummy and hips.

PERTINENT PATTERN INFORMATION

As you know, this book is about quilted garments, but don't worry if you can't find a pattern you like in this category. You can always *add* the quilting. All patterns come with printed instructions, so read these through at the beginning; this is your road map to tell you where you are going. The patterns also will have diagrams and drawings for you to follow, and they will tell you how much fabric to buy. This may not do you much good if you are planning to "make" your own fabric, but it does give you a good idea at least of how much you need. Any special sewing sequence or construction will also be detailed in your pattern; even though you might not follow it exactly, it is a good idea to read through the information, which after all has been put there to help you.

Most of the Big Four patterns come in specific sizes. If you aren't sure of the size you need, buy the same size in a pattern that you would buy in a ready-made garment. For instance, if you wear a size 12 in a ready-made, get a size 12 in a pattern. *Do not* buy a larger size simply because you plan to quilt the garment. Some of the Big Four patterns, as well as ethnic patterns, are sized for small, medium, and large; occasionally, petite sizes are included too. In general a small size includes 8 to 10, a medium size includes 12 to 14, and anything above that is large. You may want to test out the fit of these patterns early, and you should, for one size does not necessarily fit all, despite the ads that make this claim.

All pattern pieces have grain lines to help you place the pieces correctly on the fabric. The grain line is a long line with an arrow at each end; this line corresponds to the straight grain of the fabric unless otherwise marked.

The seam allowances of the Big Four patterns are standardized at five-eighths of an inch (15 mm); they are half an inch (12 mm) in Folkwear. Following Porcella's book, you can cut patterns from paper first if you like, but she advocates a bold approach and suggests you cut directly into the fabric, following instructions and adding seam allowances.

You may have to make alterations in some patterns, depending on how you're shaped. If you have chosen a straight or square-cut garment and you have a big bust, you'd better add a dart for fit. If you don't, the garment will stand away from your body, and it won't look or feel right.

If your garment has a waistline seam, check that the pattern waistline coincides with yours. You may have to shorten or lengthen the front and back bodice pieces for a better fit. You also may have to lengthen or shorten the sleeves or add to the overall length.

There is one good solution to all of these little problems, and that is to make a muslin. A muslin is simply a trial garment, cut and basted according to your pattern pieces or measurements, that enables you to try the garment on and adjust it for fit before you cut into your good fabric. I can't recommend this step too strongly. When the muslin is right for you, take out the bastings and use it for a pattern, if you like. Muslin patterns can be used over and over again since they wear longer than tissue paper.

Don't fit your muslin too snugly because the quilting and lining will need some space too. Always check that you

Plate 1. *Pieced and quilted cotton cape, with appliqués of dotted Swiss, accented with embroidery in white perle cotton. Designed and made by Ellen Mosbarger.*

Plate 2. *Detail of Ellen Mosbarger's cape.*

Plate 3. *Greek flocata, designed and made by Charlotte Patera. Reverse appliqué is used, with red and russet cotton over coarse navy homespun, stitched with turquoise perle cotton. Vest was inspired by the flocata worn in Zagori villages in Epirus, Greece.*

Plate 4. *Painted and quilted velveteen coat. Designed and made by Joy Stocksdale.*

Plate 5. *Back view of Joy Stocksdale's coat.*

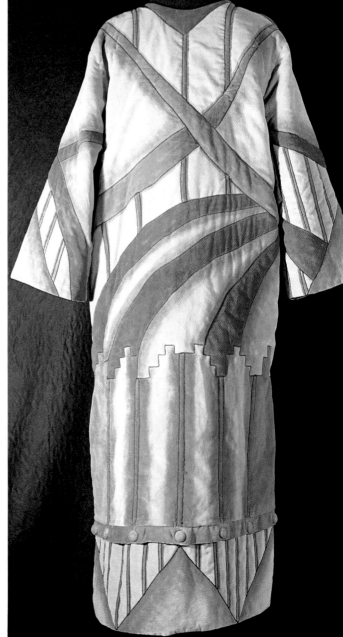

Plate 6. *Red strip-pieced cotton and cotton blend jacket, by Sue Allen Hoyt, is machine pieced and quilted, with polyester batting. Photo by Daniel Breckenridge.*

Plate 7. *Back view of shadow-quilted coat by Joy Stocksdale. Silk organza is layered over felt.*

Plate 8. *Machine-pieced and quilted jacket. Designed and made by Sue Allen Hoyt. Photo by Daniel Breckenridge.*

Plate 9. *Peacock Aurora cape, 100 percent cotton velveteen (Crompton), by Sue Allen Hoyt. Machine pieced, machine embroidered, and hand quilted with real gold (!) thread. Photo by Daniel Breckenridge.*

Plate 10. *Detail of quilting on front borders of the Peacock Aurora cape.*

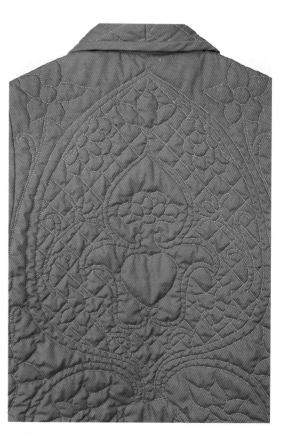

Plate 11. *Shawl collar quilted vest, by Karen Bridgewater, of red cotton. Quilting pattern was inspired by ceramic wall tile from a Persian castle dating back to the Middle Ages.*

Plate 12. *Detail of quilting on the back of Karen Bridgewater's vest.*

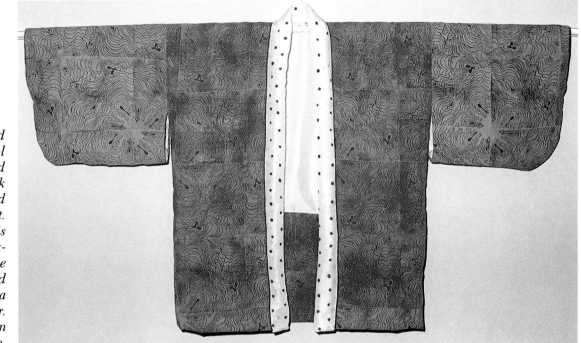

Plate 13. *Red Fields, by Carol Ward, a red and white silk Japanese quilted field jacket. Jacket body is hand block-printed, and the design is hand stamped on a rolled collar. Jacket is piped in purple cotton.*

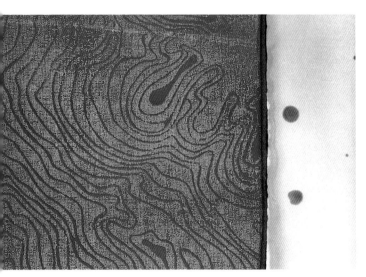

Plate 14. *Detail of Red Fields.*

Plate 15. *Becky's Coat, by Carol Ward, a child's antique silk coat with old patchwork quilt scraps (made of glosheen cotton), appliquéd on back and sleeves. Coat is trimmed with grosgrain ribbon appliqué.*

Plate 16. *Back view of Patches of Joy vest, by Joyce Kelly. Floral medallion is outline-quilted through batt and lining; the front of the vest is strip-quilted. Vest reverses to rust cotton.*

Plate 17. *Yoke of blue velveteen coat, by Kathy Murphy. Kathy's design for the people-yoke was transferred to white velveteen, hand painted with procion dyes, and then machine quilted and hand embroidered.*

Plate 18. *Another detail of the yoke of Kathy Murphy's coat. Ladies also decorate oversize cuffs.*

Plate 19. *Strip-quilted cotton jacket in various textures and shades of burgundy. Designed and made by Robin Brisco.*

Plate 20. *Square-cut cotton car coat, by Robin Brisco. Yoke and sleeves of this jacket are cut in one, and the scalloped underseam of the sleeve is lined. The sleeve edges are then tacked together to create an interesting effect. Robin quilted the garment with a feather stitch, using silk floss. Pockets were added by hand.*

Plate 21. Left: *Back view of jacket by Bonnie Case. Chintz appliqués were sewed to satin and velvet, then quilted, and metallic embroidery was added.*

Plate 22. Below: *Detail of front section of Bonnie Case's jacket.*

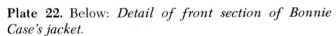

Plate 23. *Back view of jacket, by Flavin Glover, made of recycled jeans and decorated with log cabin variations in front and back panels. Photo by Glenn Glover.*

Plate 24. *Landscape Coat, by Mona Costa. Crocheted forms of perle cotton, embellished with sequins, satin ribbon, and rosebuds, were appliquéd to quilt batting and satin ground fabric. Coat was then lined with quilted peach satin.*

have enough shoulder room, especially if you want set-in sleeves. The seam of a set-in sleeve should lie comfortably over the far edge of the shoulder, where the arm joins the body; it may take a couple of try-ons as you progress with your garment, but the effort will be worthwhile because you don't want to make something that looks like it came out of the missionary box.

The Fashion Ruler, a long, curved, plastic ruler put out by Fashionetics, is a handy tool for redrawing lines when you have to alter a pattern

Also, aside from or along with muslin (and I'm talking about the good old unbleached kind), there are other pattern fabrics worth knowing about. Trace-a-pattern, by Stacy Fabrics, is one; thin Pellon is another; and a third is Do-Sew, a product from Stretch and Sew similar to Trace-a-pattern. (In the U.K. thin Vilene is the most suitable alternative.) These are pressed materials, and all make durable patterns. You can write and draw on them, which helps a lot when you are figuring out your design, especially since these materials are transparent.

Any time you spend early in the game working out the little hitches in a pattern will pay off in the future. When you've finished, you'll have a pattern that fits. It will look good and feel great, and you can use it over and over again.

Poiret contributed handsomely to the liberation of women. He threw away their corsets and stays and forced everyone in the fashion world to accept the shape of women's bodies as they were. He recognized how marvelously supple they were, what truly wonderful natural machines they were, and he made clothes to fit and flow over them. You can too. Know thyself.

3

FABRICS: FEELING THE GOODS

Choosing fabric, or a combination of fabrics, is possibly the most important decision you will make; it determines the life or death of your garment. Exquisite fabric flawlessly constructed is perfection itself. You could write a poem about some of the elegant fabrics available. The pattern style must take second place in any such decision, for it is the fabric that catches the eye, as well as the mind and heart. Most often fabric dictates style, and, again, the simpler the better. Your garment can be all of one fabric, or, by combining several in color and design—by piecing in various forms, or by applying design as in appliqué, or by painting, silk screening, or anything you like—you can literally create your own fabric. Experiment with classes and instruction books on hand painting and screening and batiking fabrics to find out how deep the appeal is for you. In this book I am emphasizing the threaded needle, whether hand or machine and whether plain stitching, quilting, or embroidery. One or more or all of these devices together provide endless opportunity to create unusual effects with fabric.

In addition to discussing fabrics in this chapter, we will also examine texture and color; they all go together, and there isn't any way you can separate them. As with love and marriage, which "go together like a horse and carriage," you can't have fabric without texture and color.

There is not only a staggering wealth of fabrics available to us but also an equally staggering amount of research; we might learn more about fabrics than we care to know. Here we're going to concentrate on woven fabrics, since the garments we make will be quilted. That doesn't mean you can't quilt knits, because you can. But you will have to deal with a built-in stretch, since that's what knits are all about. (I have seen some stunning quilted knit garments. Marjorie Puckett used a prequilted knit to make a fitted evening jacket, trimmed with ribbon ruching around the neck and sleeves. (See the photo on page 115.)

There are roughly two classes of fabrics—natural and synthetic. Nothing, to my mind, can take the place of or even compare with natural fibers. Their sewing and wearing qualities are unsurpassed, though synthetic fibers and blends certainly get an A for effort.

Natural fibers live and breathe. They keep us cool in summer and warm in winter. In any season and any climate, they offer us the ultimate in body comfort. They are also expensive and becoming more so all the time, though, and they are not as plentiful as they used to be. Scarcity and cost are two factors that have encouraged the manufacture of synthetic fibers; the various types and combinations have also given us undreamed-of types and textures. These are not all substitutions for natural fabrics, but they stand on their own for handling and wearability. Many are highly acceptable, as competition gets keener and quality control becomes more demanding. Sometimes it is difficult to tell a "fake" silk or wool from the real thing; at least, I find it so. Often synthetic fibers are added to natural fibers to strengthen them, or perhaps to make them wrinkle-free. At any rate, they're here to stay.

Natural woven—or knit—fabrics fall easily into four categories: silk, cotton, linen, and wool. All four come in many weights and many textures, and almost all have a counterpart among the synthetics. The names we hear most often are polyester, acrylic, orlon, nylon, and rayon.

WEIGHT

We can also classify fabrics, roughly, into three other groups—thin, medium, and heavy weights. Thin fabrics are usually transparent or semitransparent. They include batiste, chiffon, organdy, organza, voile, dotted swiss, and sometimes challis. Many delicate silks and polyesters may also fit into the thin category, or lightweight fabric class, even though they may not be transparent. All such fabrics can be quilted but probably should be quilted by hand because they are so delicate. A floaty chiffon can be used as an overlay or shadow fabric with an opaque one, or it can be used over felt, flannel, or a thin batt. There aren't any blanket rules that cover their use; each decision must be made separately considering the fabric, filler, design, and technique—but that's what makes a quilted garment so exciting to make and wear.

Mediumweight fabrics include muslin, broadcloth, flannel, satin, raw silk, wool crepe, worsteds, some linens, and many of the synthetic mixtures marketed under fancy names. Good old-fashioned unbleached muslin is one of the best fabrics ever produced, for it is endlessly versatile. It is a bedrock basic for quiltmaking, but it works for garments too. As a rule we use mediumweight fabrics in quiltmaking; broadcloths, either natural cotton or a blend, and prints are standards. For wall quilts we add satins and polished cottons and sometimes velveteen, velvet, and corduroy.

Usually the mediumweight fabrics we use in making bed quilts, the ones we actually sleep under, are washable and, in fact, have been washed before we start to work on them. This is a precaution against shrinkage. It is also something you don't have to do when you make a quilted garment unless you want to. Unbleached muslin is about the only fabric I insist on washing, and I do that automatically because it shrinks so much, even when dry cleaned. I don't prewash any other fabrics unless they're dirty or they have a horrible smell to them—is it formaldehyde they use in finishing some fabrics? Whatever it is, I'd probably wash anything that had that smell. Sometimes washing takes the sheen from polished cotton and the sizing from others; I want the sheen of polished cotton to stay put, and I think the sizing in fabrics often helps in appliqué and quilting both. Many times too, in making a garment, you use a mixture of fabrics, many of which could not be washed. I have most of my quilted garments dry cleaned and hope you do too; even if the fabrics are washable, such garments need professional pressing. Test dark solids for bleeding.

Wools come in many weights. The light-to-medium weights are wonderful to work with in garments, and most quilt easily and show off well. They can be combined with cottons and linens, velvets, satins, and corduroys, leather, suede, and Ultrasuede fabric, or they can be used alone. In today's dressing we seldom use heavyweight fabrics unless for sportswear or outdoor clothes. A heavy fabric with added batt and lining might be too heavy to wear with comfort; this is an individual decision and depends entirely on the components used.

Combining weights is also a possibility in making a garment, but if there is too much difference in the weights (and, therefore, the handling) of the fabrics, you may have to back or stabilize a thinner fabric before incorporating it with a heavier one.

TEXTURE

One of the most important aspects of fabric, as important as the fibers, is the texture. Smooth or rough, shiny or matte, they all have appeal. Most cotton broadcloths have a smooth, matte finish; polished cotton has a sheen. Satin also has a sheen; and velvet and velveteen have depth. The dull finishes or textures absorb light, and the bright finishes reflect it. Nap or pile fabrics have a definite direction. Most of the time you cut and sew them with the pile going in one direction (usually down), but you can achieve wonderful effects by deliberately changing the direction of the pile or ribs, as in corduroy. These fabrics can be used separately or in combination with others; an exciting experiment is to combine unlikely fabrics and textures. You never know what will happen until you try it. Most of these fabrics can also be quilted, but be sure to try some samples first. You don't want quilting lines to be lost in a nubby texture or deep pile.

NOVEL OR UNUSUAL MATERIALS

There are certain materials that should not be overlooked for quilted garments. Felt, thin leathers, suede, Ultrasuede fabric and some vinyl or coated fabrics can all be quilted and because of their texture and makeup are easier to quilt by machine. These materials also may need stabilizing as you sew or quilt them. Tissue or tracing paper on the bottom next to the feed plate is best, and the paper can be torn away when the sewing or quilting is finished.

Try to achieve as much variety as possible in your fabric stockpile. The same shade in different textures, graduated shades of the same weave, assorted prints—all of these have a place. When you see an unusual piece, be it large or small, and are attracted to it, buy it. Sooner or later you will find a use for it.

COLOR

There is no way to divorce fiber from texture, just as there is no way to divorce fiber from color. "No-color" begins with white and leads to beige and natural earth tones, then to browns, grays, and finally, black. New modern dyes have raised color sense to a more sophisticated level; there seems to be no end to the choice. With all of this selection, several friends of mine prefer to dye their own fabrics to get a certain shade or a blending of shades, and you may want to experiment with dyeing too. I find such bewildering arrays confronting me in fabric shops that I go no further. Solid colors, or tone-on-tones, are manufactured in a complete range. So are the prints, or designed fabrics. There are plaids, stripes, checks, and dots—all of them ranging from tiny to large. There are the tiny all-over print calicos so familiar to quilters, and there are florals, large or small and precise or abstract. There are also geometric prints, pattern on-pattern motifs, paisleys, and interesting border-printed fabrics.

When combining fabrics, large-scaled or asymmetrical designs are often very interesting to work with because each time you cut into the fabric it looks different. It is also possible to use the wrong side of these fabrics; you get the same colors, the same designs, but softer and fainter for the most part. It's like having two fabrics for the price of one.

Many people feel unsure of themselves when they are making decisions about color. I don't know very much about color theory, but I rely on my instincts and intuitions. Several well-known quilters do too, and I mention this to give you confidence. Long ago I found that the color of a fabric often does not look like the color on a chart or the color of paper, so I work directly with the fabric. Photo 5 shows a good color chart made by Fashionetics, and it may help you in sorting out different color areas.

A good exercise to learn about fabrics is to pick up a handful of goods. Start with solid colors, and take a good look at them to see how they look and interact together. Pin them on a wall or lay them on the floor, and then step back and squint. Put the little pile of fabrics next to a piece of black fabric, and then put them next to a piece of white to check out the difference. The eye is easy to educate, and soon you will know what combination is exactly right for your project, or whether something is missing, and the color scheme hasn't quite come together.

Color wheels can be purchased in almost any fabric or art supply store, and it might help if you studied one. The basis of a wheel is really an equilateral triangle, each of the points being one of the three primary hues—red, blue, and yellow. Mix two of these together in equal parts and you get secondary colors—purple, green, and orange.

5. *Color wheel. The Fashion Co-ordinator*^{TM} *by Fashionetics, Inc.*

Value is another property of color. It refers to dark and light. If you add black to a hue, you get a darker value. If you add white, you get a lighter value. If you wanted to use a wide range of reds in your work, you would be using a range of values—or shades—since the hue is limited.

Intensity is also a property of color. An intense color is bold and brilliant, but if you add other hues to it, especially its opposite on the color wheel, some of the intensity is lost;

6. *Samurai vest, designed and made by Jo Ann Giordano, back view. (See Plate 38 for front view.) The idea for the vest is based on Japanese Samurai armor. The vest is made from satins and other fabrics.*

the color becomes duller, more muted. The more you "play" with your fabrics, the more you'll learn about color, what it can do for you, and what you can do for it.

I must confess to an identity problem with color in the past several years, and this is due directly to the advertising world. In ready-to-wear, cosmetics, and home decorations, colors have assumed new identities. Green is no longer just green. It is kelly, spring, poison, pistachio, sweet apple, mustard, loden, or olive. Red is fire engine, real, blush, wild plum, burgundy, cranberry, rose, wicked pink, or brick. No wonder we're confused.

William Accorsi sums up color better than anyone I know. He wrote a delightful book, *Accorsi Puzzles*, in which he says:

> The first color is red. Red was invented by a Spaniard who was a chemist and as a hobby did bull fighting. He used it on his cape and got bulls madder than anyone else. The second color is blue—blue was found lying around on the ground by Mr. DaVinci when he was searching for purple. Another color is yellow. No one knows who really discovered yellow. Red—yellow—blue, I think that is about it except for black and white.

You said it, William!

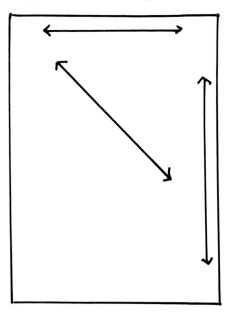

Fig. 4. *Grain lines for patterns and fabrics. Horizontal arrow is crosswise grain or warp; vertical arrow is lengthwise grain or woof; diagonal arrow is bias grain.*

GRAIN

Every sewer and quilter knows you can't fool around with grain. It's there and you've got to do something about it. If you "go against the grain," you will pay for it in one way or another. Grain refers to the warp and woof of woven fabrics. The woof is the crosswise thread, and the warp is the lengthwise thread. These two should cross each other at right angles. The threads along the outside edges are interwoven tightly, and this edge is called the selvedge. If fabrics aren't on grain when you buy them, you'll have to straighten them when you get home. Fabrics are rolled on tubes or wound on flat boards (paper, not wood) by machine at the finishing mill; this process, if off by the slightest fraction, can result in the whole bolt of fabric being off grain by the time it gets to the store. It isn't always easy to see, but it is easy enough to check, and you *should* check it, because the grain of the fabric must be straight if you want a good-looking garment. Fabric hangs or drapes according to the grain and the way it was cut; if you cut your garment off grain, it will hang crooked for as long as it lives.

First you have to straighten the crosswise grain. This is the width of the fabric. The easiest way to do this is to tear the fabric, but try it first on a small section at the end. Some fabrics won't tear without ruffling or stretching the edge, and you don't want this. Some fabrics won't tear at all. If they will, go ahead and tear a strip across; the tear will be absolutely true along the crosswise grain. You can also pull a thread to straighten the grain, although you probably will be able to pull only a couple of inches at a time before the thread breaks. The thread will leave a tiny ladderlike line in the fabric; you cut along this line to the point where the thread broke, then pull some more. Repeat the process across the width of the fabric.

Once the crosswise edge is straight, fold the fabric in the middle lengthwise, matching up the raw edges of the width, and pin at the selvedges. Pin across the top, keeping the raw edges even, and then begin to pin down the selvedge edge. If the folded fabric lies absolutely flat, the grain is straight, and you can go out and celebrate. If there is a diagonal pull or wrinkle and the fabric buckles, then you have a little job ahead of you.

Get someone to help you, and pull the fabric diagonally from opposite corners. If the wrinkles persist, you'll need to dampen the fabric and work or pull it until all the wrinkles

7. *"Chinese Lightning Vest," designed and made by Jo Ann Giordano. This vest is cotton sateen hand screened with an image of atomic particle tracks and a geometric pattern superimposed on this. It is machine quilted and is trimmed with heavy braid around the neck.*

come out and the fabric lies flat. Keep the fabric envelope pinned or basted, roll it in a dampened sheet and leave it for an hour or two, then pull diagonally again and smooth the fabric with your hands. You may need to press after this; use a press cloth and a good steam iron set at the proper temperature.

The straight grain, both crosswise and lengthwise, is firm, with little give except in loosely woven fabrics. It is the bias grain that has the stretch, and that is good or bad, depending on how you handle it. I consider it a plus because the cling and drape of bias is beautiful to behold, and you can manipulate all kinds of effects with it. It follows the line of the body with grace and often you can use a pattern designed for straight-grain cutting, change it to bias, and have something unusual and very special.

HOW MUCH FABRIC TO BUY

This is a very iffy problem, and there may be a dozen different solutions, all depending on the fabric or fabrics you plan to use. If you want to make a quilted garment using one fabric for the shell and another for the lining, then you can usually go by the fabric chart on the pattern. If you are piecing your own fabric, however, it's another story. I don't like to get into the mathematics; I much prefer to have a selection of fabrics on hand without concern as to whether they are in half- or full-yard lengths and put them together; if I run out of something, another fabric may be substituted, often with an unexpected but pleasing effect.

If you want to bind all the seams and outside edges with your own fabric, buy an extra yard; this should be quite enough, perhaps with a little left over. If you are appliquéing designs over one chosen fabric, then again, follow the pattern instructions. If you are piecing the shell and then adding appliqué, you will have to figure differently. Also, if the body of the garment is to be of one fabric and the sleeves and front band or binding of another, you have another set of figures to juggle. Therefore, buy plenty—more than you think you'll need; you can always use it.

WHERE TO BUY FABRIC

It seems silly, in a way, to talk about sources for most of us have our favorite shops. Not all carry the same lines, however, so it does pay to look around. Some stores deal entirely with natural fibers; others with fabrics imported from countries that specialize in certain textures or designs. Some fabrics suitable for clothes can be found in slipcover and

8. *"Apricot and Mocha," designed and made by Marilyn Price. This Folkwear Turkish coat is hand-dyed, hand-printed cotton velveteen and machine quilted.*

upholstery departments. Many fine and unusual fabrics can be ordered through the mail. Thrift shops are a possibility, but you should check fabrics you are considering to be sure they are not too worn. Often you can cut and save the good, usable parts. Often, too, thrift shops carry lengths of fabrics that have never been used for one reason or another. Now and then I have given fabric to our local thrift store, so I know. I do this reluctantly, with the final recognition that I will probably never cut into or sew this fabric, although my early intentions were otherwise.

Antique shops and flea markets are wonderful sources of fabrics, and you may stumble on a real find. Even table cloths, shawls, scarves, and remnants can be incorporated into a stunning garment, combined with new fabrics you have on hand. Men's ties are a source we should not over-look. Many of them are made of heavy woven silk; if you take the tie apart, the wrong side may be as fresh and new looking as the tie was at the beginning; these heavy silks are wonderful for certain types of patchwork.

Most people who work with fabrics, including myself, are also obsessed with having stacks and stacks of them. I seldom go into a fabric shop without seeing something I just can't live without. I am also guilty of buying impulsively—too impulsively. There have been times when a sale price influenced my decision, and most of the time I've regretted this, unless it happened to be a fabric I'd wanted for some time. A markdown or sale price certainly is a temptation, but it should by no means be the deciding factor in a purchase.

Storage is always a problem. I want to see my fabrics and not have to rummage around in boxes or drawers, but this is not always possible. Most of my fabrics are on open shelves, but there are also a lot in boxes; I number or write on these boxes and then try to keep an inventory list or cross-index. I check the list for the contents of the box and where it is (under the table, on the floor of the closet, on the closet shelf in the next room).

When you're choosing fabrics for that smashing quilted garment you want to make, stretch your imagination a little. Put colors and textures together in a new and different combination, play with them, abandon yourself to them. Julia Child urges her cooks along the same lines, to play with their food:

> Play to me means freedom and delight, as in the phrase "play of imagination." If cooks did not enjoy speculating about new possibilities in every method and each raw material, their art would stagnate and they would become rote performers, not creators. True cooks love to set one flavor against another in their imagination, to experiment with the great wealth of fresh produce in the supermarkets, to bake what previously they braised, to try new devices. We all have flops, of course, but we learn from them; and when an invention or a variation works out at last, it is an enormous pleasure to propose it to our fellows.
>
> Let's all play with our food, I say, and, in so doing, let us advance the state of the art together.*

Play with your fabrics and your designs; set one technique against another. Experiment with the wealth of color and texture we have at hand; when your garment is finished, it will be unique, your personal individual interpretation, and you will have enormous pleasure in sharing it with others.

Godspeed.

*From *Julia Child and Company*, by Julia Child. New York: Alfred A. Knopf, Inc., 1978. Reprinted by permission of the publisher.

4

DEVELOPING DESIGN: BY CHANGING PATTERN LINE AND BY PIECING

Design seems to be the true hang-up for most people, and its pursuit is often accompanied by gnashing of teeth and great frustration. Design is all around us—we live in a world of it—yet often it seems elusive. We just need to remind ourselves of a few simple truths, however. To be effective, a design does not need to be intricate or elaborate. Some of the most stunning are the simplest. Actually, in one way or another all the elements of design are spread out in front of us; you're free to dip in and take what you want or need. There is really no such thing as *original* design—the word should be *unique* instead—but *your* design comes from the bits and pieces you choose, the way you put them together, and whether you want your design to come from style, from color, from texture, or from a combination of all three. We want our work to be different and to express our views, attitudes, and approaches. And we want the recognition of those people whose judgment we consider valid and sound.

We also need to open up to the world around us—to see and hear and touch. Inspiration often lurks in unexpected places, and we must be ready for it. We see the way the light hits the side of a building and creates a design in shadow. We read a quotation or a passage that evokes a visual image that can be translated into fabric. We see a photograph, a painting, a sculpture, a magazine illustration, or an advertisement; any of these can set creative juices flowing. You can help by keeping a notebook or a file; unrecorded ideas are often lost and gone forever. Once you get in the habit of using it, and once you begin to *see* what goes on around you, the ideas will begin to tumble over themselves, each clamoring for attention. Design, or inspiration, is an evolving process, not an instant commodity. We all read about writers who sit down to the typewriter and write marvelous articles and books without hesitation. We hear of the artist who snatches up his brushes, rushes to the easel, and turns out a masterpiece in record time. Or the high fashion designer who throws a length of fabric so unerringly over a model's shoulder that women clutch at her as she goes down the runway. All of these achievements are simply the final result of trial and error, of adding and subtracting, of accepting and rejecting, and of continually trying out new combinations of elements, a new and different approach to a familiar, traditional, and time-worn premise.

9. *Back view of a machine-quilted bright blue cotton jacket striped with orange and red piecing, designed and made by Harriet Thornton.*

THE PATTERN AS DESIGN

Once you've chosen your pattern for a garment, you can leave it as is or change the style. Even small changes in a pattern can give it a unique or unexpected look. In Chapter 2 we talked about changing a pattern for fit. Now let's think about changing it for style.

1. Eliminate a seam. If there is a center back seam, or side back or side seam, think about cutting the fabric in one piece and eliminating one or more seams. This will change the drape of the garment somewhat, but it may be just what you're after.
2. Add back flare. Take a pattern with a straight, center-back seam: measure two inches (5 cm) out from the center back seam line at bottom of garment, and mark the place on fabric or paper. With a ruler, draw a line from this mark to the center back neck seam. This seam will then be on the bias, and there will be an added four inches (10 cm) of flare in the center of the back section.
3. Add pleats or gathers to the cap of a set-in sleeve or to the top of a dropped-shoulder sleeve.
4. Change the front closing. If your garment closes down the center front, move the closure to one side. Or make an asymmetrical closing for the front pattern sections.

5. Change a wrapped garment. The Folkwear Turkish coat pattern (*see Photo 8*) with its front band is an example of changing a wrapped garment. The band goes all the way around the neck and creates a kind of collar. I wanted to widen the right front band and give it a sweeping look for the coat "Lightning Strikes Twice" (*see Plates 64 and 65*). I pinned the front band pattern to the front coat section of the original pattern, matching up the seamlines. Then I pinned paper I could see through over this and redrew the front band as I wanted it. I used this paper pattern when I cut out the fabric.

6. Change the neckline. One of the obvious ways to change a pattern is at the neckline. You can add a collar if there is none or eliminate it if the pattern does have a collar. You can also change the style of the collar or replace it with a ruffle or a scarf. In the body of a garment it is possible to add a yoke either to the front or back.

Remember whenever you make significant changes in a pattern, it's a good idea to make a note on the pattern envelope, or a slip of paper inside, specifying what you've done.

Although to me fabric outweighs pattern in importance, many times the lines and style of a pattern are so appealing that that consideration comes first. Some coat and jacket patterns truly have nine lives—made up in the proper fabric and quilted, they can be worn for sports, evening, business, and, in fact, almost any occasion.

DESIGN THROUGH PIECING

Either the shell or the lining or both of a quilted garment may be pieced. Either also may be quilted separately, or they can be quilted together in a quilt-as-you-go fashion. As in most design areas, the variations of piecing are endless, but the approach is a little different. You aren't just piecing blocks as you would for a quilt; you are planning a design that will fit the pattern sections of your garment. This can be an all-over design, or it can be highlighted in specific places—for example, on sleeves or front band. You can do simple piecing by joining squares, rectangles, or triangles to create a design or a length of fabric. You can do the same with hexagons or diamonds or use a design calling for curved piecing. You can join different pieces of fabric together at random, much like the old crazy-patchwork, or you can piece wide strips of fabric together and use them vertically or horizontally. You can also cut narrow strips of fabric, strips of varying widths (even or uneven), or wedge-shaped pieces and stitch them together to make your design. Such classic piecing as the log cabin design adapts beautifully to garments, as does Seminole patchwork. The choice is yours.

10a. *"Purse Jacket," by Robin Brisco. This black and white quilted cotton jacket has seven concealed pockets, designed to hold things ordinarily carried in a purse. The pockets are finished with topstitched grosgrain ribbon and close with Velcro.*

10b. *Back view of "Purse Jacket."*

Most piecing is better done on the machine than by hand; the work is faster and also stronger. Since the thread won't show, it doesn't need to match, so this is a good opportunity to use up all the odds and ends you have lying around. I use the quilter's seam allowance when I piece fabrics for garments—one-quarter of an inch (6 mm). My presser foot is a quarter of an inch from needle to edge, and it serves as a guide in keeping the seams even. Measure the distance of your needle to presser foot edge before you start, and it may help too to put a strip of masking tape on the right side of the machine bed for stitching an even seam.

When you have a general idea of what you want to do, make a tracing of your pattern on another piece of paper, and use this tracing to work out your design. This way you aren't cluttering up your original pattern with lines and drawings you won't want there forever. Also, if you change your mind—and I often do—it's easier to work out the changes on a duplicate pattern.

The square is perhaps the mother of all geometric shapes. You can divide it into smaller squares, rectangles, or traingles or cut off the corners to make a hexagon. From a square you can also create circles, diamonds, and parallelograms. All those quilt block patterns you have in books, magazines, and your pattern files are a wonderful source of ideas. Although they may have been planned for quilt blocks, they can easily be lifted out of block form and used for a garment section. Also, you need not use the complete block design—perhaps only part of it or half will give you the lines you want. Try enlarging it by several sizes; larger pieces are easier to work with, and larger spaces give you greater opportunity for quilting. If you have some leftover quilt blocks, or if you like the pattern so much you want to use it block-form in a garment, then consider using blocks down the center back, across the shoulders, or on each sleeve. A quilt block cut in two diagonally or on the straight offers another type of design.

A very good example of using a quilt-block design in a garment is the cape made by Lesly-Claire Greenberg (*Plate 43*), cut in a half-circle. The design is based on the mariner's compass quilt pattern, radial piecing that is dramatic and effective.

Choose one or two quilt-block patterns you like and try them out. Don't be discouraged if they aren't as successful as you thought they would be; you've still learned something. I learn more from my disasters than I do from my triumphs. Here are some other suggestions that may help you:

1. Create your own yardage by piecing together squares or rectangles. This is the simplest form of piecing, but the fabric choices can make it very distinctive. Pieces may be of the same size or graduated. For example, an eight-

11. *Quilted jacket, back view, by Helen Richards. The fabric is cotton, strip pieced in shades of red and rust, using solid colors and silk-screened Finnish fabrics. The design is limited deliberately by fabric selection.*

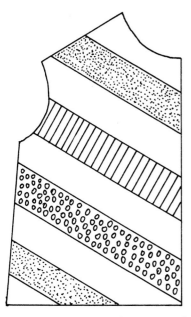

Fig. 5a. *An example of simple diagonal strip piecing.*

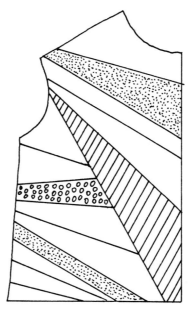

Fig. 5b. *Piecing variation.*

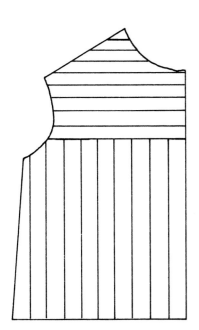

Fig. 5c. *Horizontal and vertical strip piecing combined.*

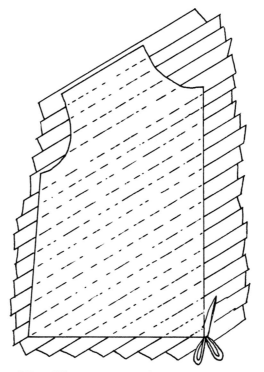

Fig. 5d. *Diagram shows the wrong side of foundation fabric or paper used in strip piecing. When seaming is finished, the edges of the strips are trimmed to pattern size.*

Fig. 6. *Pieced design using diagonally split quilt block as a focal point on vest or jacket front.*

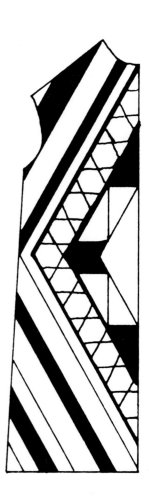

inch (20-cm) square could be pieced to an eight-inch block composed of smaller squares. Four- or five-inch (10- or 13-cm) squares are a good size to use as a working unit, although any size is acceptable; it depends on how much piecing you want to do. Remember, fabric is the key; you can use all solids or solids combined with prints, or you can combine all prints. Sections of pieced squares can also be broken up with "sashing"—the same kind you use in piecing a quilt.

2. Try diamonds or hexagons pieced together for an all-over design. Increase the size of the shape for easier piecing; also, experiment with the hexagon—split it and use two different fabrics when you join the two sections, or use two shades of one fabric.

3. Curved piecing is exciting and dramatic, especially when combined with straight-line piecing. Try developing a design of your own using a compass and a ruler. Curved seams can be stitched easily on the machine, and without stay-stitching. Use the quarter-inch seam allowance, and be precise about matching up the beginning and end of the seam line. You are working with two opposite curves—convex and concave, or outside and inside curves—and stitching them together is easier than you think. There is enough bias stretch in each curve to meet the common seam line; after you have matched up the beginning and end of each seam and pinned them so they won't slip, you can match the raw edges of the curves, pin them, and away you go. Don't try to press these seams open; press them to the side. With curves you should be able to press without clipping; with a straight seam, press toward the darker fabric.

4. Random piecing. This is very similar to crazy-patchwork, but without the embroidery over the seams. Not that you can't use embroidery because you can; embroidery gives a charming Victorian appearance to your work, especially if you have used fabrics we associate with this type of piecing: dark velvets, brocades, silks, and ribbons. You can use any fabrics in random piecing,

Fig. 7. Spiderweb design, an old pieced quilt pattern, lends itself to strip piecing in garments too.

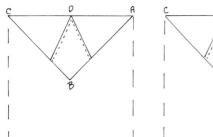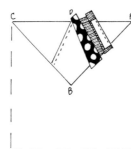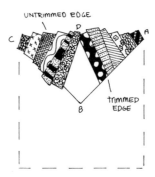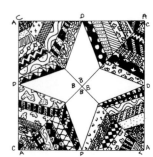

12a. *Hand-quilted jacket of black polished cotton with Fairfield Cotton Classic filler, by Sonya Barrington. The jacket is "Eisenhower" or bomber-style with black and white checkerboard strips stitched diagonally down the front. The jacket fastens with loops and Chinese ball buttons.*

12b. *Back view of "Eisenhower" or bomber-style jacket.*

putting color against color, texture against texture. You can work directly with your fabric, trimming and stitching as you go, or you may want to draw a design on your duplicate pattern section first and then cut paper templates to use with your fabric.

5. Strip or string piecing is one of the most exciting and challenging areas of all. The technique goes back to the beginning of quiltmaking in this country, when thrifty quiltmakers used every scrap they could get their hands on, down to the tiniest "string" in the scrap bag. Fabric artists today have raised strip piecing to new, sophisticated levels—and with great success. Strips can be any width, any color, and they do not need to be even; it depends on whether you want a balanced design or not. You can create yardage with string piecing and cut out pattern sections when the piecing is done. You can also use string piecing in certain sections for emphasis— bands of it sandwiched in between solid colors, on sleeves, around hems, or down the front closing of a garment. You can use your yardage as over-all fabric, or you can cut shapes from it and piece these together for a complex design.

Don't confuse string piecing with string quilting; they are not the same. When you are string piecing, you are seaming strips of fabric together. You do not always need a foundation fabric for this; just cut your strings or strips, stitch them together with the quarter-inch seam, and press. If you are sewing thin or slippery fabrics, use tissue or tracing paper underneath to stabilize the stitching and keep the seams smooth, then tear the paper away later.

When you get ready to stitch, be sure your thread selection is right for the fabric. Then choose the needle to go with the thread and test out tensions and stitch lengths before you start.

If you want to use a foundation fabric for random piecing, crazy-patchwork, or string work, choose a very lightweight woven fabric, such as batiste. It is firm enough to hold the work in place and light enough not to interfere with quilting.

6. Seminole Patchwork. This unique form of pieced design comes from the Seminole Indians of Florida. Quilters and home sewers alike know a good thing when they see it and have experimented endlessly with it, developing new designs of their own. It looks far more difficult than it is. Long, even strips of fabric are seamed together to form a band. After pressing, the band is cut into sections and reseamed by dropping or offsetting one or more sections. When the cuts are straight, the little sections are reseamed in a staggered or flipped pattern.

13a. *Back view of "Bedding in Kimono Form," designed and made by Yvonne Porcella. Strip pieced of thirty-five fabrics and highlighted with black and white triangle bands, the kimono is designed to be worn as outerwear or sleepwear or to be hung on the wall. Photo by Elaine F. Keenan.*

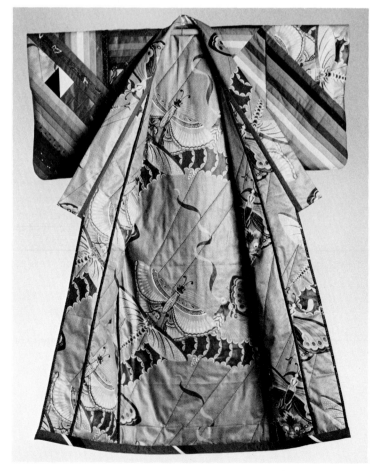

13b. *Front view shows kimono displayed in traditional Japanese manner. It is lined with kite-printed fabric and hand quilted from the lining side following kite-string lines of fabric. Photo by Elaine F. Keenan.*

Fig. 8. *Basic Seminole patchwork.*

a. *Contrasting fabric strips are seamed together to make a band.*

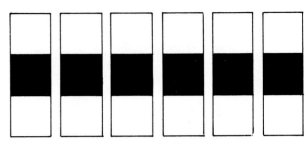

b. *Band is cut apart in even segments. This is called "straight cut."*

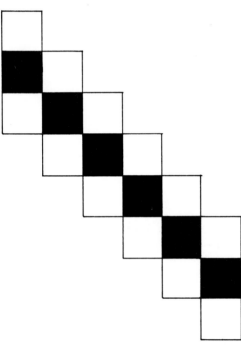

c. *Cuts are seamed together, offset by width of one fabric strip.*

d. *Completed Seminole design. Dotted lines show where design is to be joined to plain strips or garment sections.*

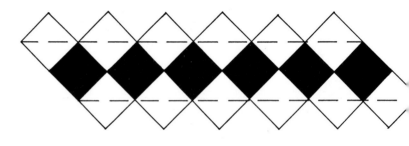

When the cuts are at an angle, they too can be seamed together in staggered fashion or flipped (turning every other section upside down) to make zigzag patterns. When half of the bands are cut mirror image or in reverse and then stitched together, they form a herringbone pattern.

These bands, each with a different design, were used to decorate men's and women's jackets and women's skirts. A good jacket might incorporate four bands. It is absolutely essential to tear or cut your fabric strips on the grain, or you will mess up the entire design. Some fabrics can be torn successfully, and I see no reason why you shouldn't do so if tearing doesn't stretch the edges of the fabric. A crosswise tear is on grain, and it does save time in marking and measuring.

If you prefer to cut strips, you can cut many instead of one. Press your fabric, then stack up to eight or nine

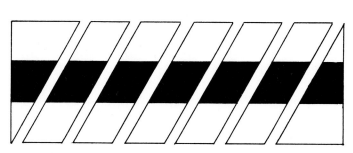

e. *Same basic band as in Fig. a, but now cut at an angle instead of straight.*

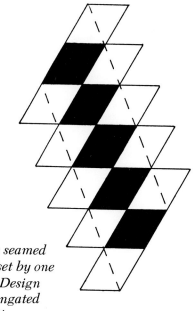

f. *Angle cuts seamed together, offset by one fabric strip. Design makes an elongated diamond pattern.*

g. *Original band (a) folded for cutting. One half will be cut as usual, the other cut in reverse for a mirror-image design.*

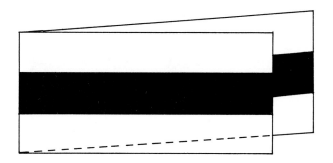

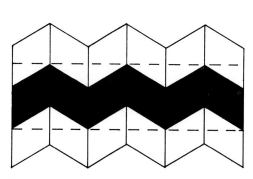

h. *Cuts are alternated as they are seamed, making a herringbone or zigzag Seminole mirror-image design.*

layers together. Be sure that you line up the raw edges of fabric widths evenly and that you do the same with the selvedges. Pin these layers together securely so that they won't slip. Mark your cutting lines with a ruler or other strip-marking device, and then cut. Gingher shears will cut easily through this many layers of fabric.

The Olfa rotary cutter is also excellent for this purpose. When the fabrics are pinned together, put them on the self-sealing cutting surface. You can also fold the fabric widths into fourths, pin to secure, then cut. The cutting line does not need to be marked in advance because the cutter rides along the edge of a see-through plastic ruler. Both of these methods are great time-savers.

Bands or strips of Seminole work can add immeasurably to the design of a quilted garment, but it would be not only difficult but needless to try to quilt the bands themselves. There are too many seams, and the design needs no further enhancing. I used a strip of Seminole piecing down one sleeve of "Lightning Strikes Twice" (*Plates 64 and 65*), a black machine-quilted coat with red sleeves.

7. Log Cabin Piecing. This is another familiar pieced design that dates back to the beginning of quiltmaking but also adapts very well to clothing. Log cabin blocks can be made any size and used in parts of a garment or as an all-over design. Blocks are made up of half light and half dark fabrics, and it is possible to combine these in any number of ways. In recent years many quilters and fabric artists have experimented with log cabin work too, creating off-center designs and changing the widths of the "logs."

Many of you reading this book have had a lot of experience in piecing, but I want to list a few guidelines or re-

Fig. 9. *Steps in constructing a log cabin block. Such blocks are often used in pieced designs for quilted garments, from small units seamed together to large designs that cover most of garment or pattern area.*

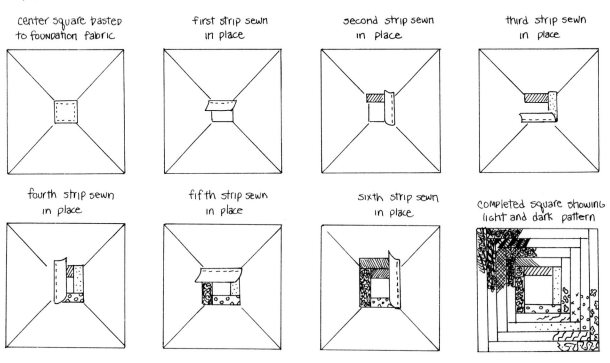

center square basted to foundation fabric — first strip sewn in place — second strip sewn in place — third strip sewn in place

fourth strip sewn in place — fifth strip sewn in place — sixth strip sewn in place — completed square showing light and dark pattern

minders for those of you who want to explore this further.

Grain plays an important part in cutting and piecing. Squares and rectangles should be cut on the straight grain for easy sewing. A hexagon and diamond both have two sides on the straight grain; the others are bias. Often you can control the stretch in the bias by stitching one bias side to the straight side of another piece.

If you have trouble stitching curves together, stay-stitch the inside curve, then clip through the seam allowance at right angles to the stitching line. This is a technique we use frequently in appliqué work; if you practice seaming curves together without stay-stitching, using the suggestions given earlier, you will probably find that you can handle them very well.

There are instruction books written specifically for Seminole, log cabin, and other piecing; check the bibliography for details. If you use the dining room or kitchen table as a work table, a cutting board, available at most fabric shops, is a big help. It not only protects the table top but helps you align your fabric on grain, following the printed lines on the board.

Remember, too, that no pieced design, no matter how cleverly planned or drawn, will look right unless the right fabrics are chosen for it. Be receptive and open to everything, and many times you will get an inspiration from something you've overlooked before. Try combining fabrics you think don't belong together; sometimes you are happily surprised. And remember that large prints and border fabrics, as well as others, can be cut out of context. Striped fabrics offer exciting variety for pieced work, as do special bits and pieces, the old quilt block, a piece of embroidery or hand-painted silk, perhaps a width of Japanese obi cloth, or scraps of batik. *Play* with your fabrics to create your pieced design.

I've emphasized machine piecing in this chapter, but that certainly does not mean you can't do your piecing by hand if you prefer. I suggest you stick to machine for strip or Seminole work, but any other piecing is as easily done by hand as it is by machine. Handpiecing is also portable; you can accomplish a lot when you take it with you. You can also do hand work with your feet propped up while you watch television. Put everything you need—needle and thread, thimble and scissors, fabric and pattern pieces—in a plastic bag, then they are ready when you are.

Remember also to press. Press fabrics before you cut for piecing if the fabric is wrinkled. Wrinkled fabric is impossible to cut accurately. Also press your fabric when the piecing is finished. One thing I learned years ago in sewing was "Don't sew over an unpressed seam." That rule is still valid.

5

DEVELOPING
DESIGN:
WITH
APPLIQUÉ

By now you know the wonderful possibilities of design when you piece the shell or lining of a garment. There are equally as many—if not more—marvelous opportunities when you choose appliqué as your medium of expression. You can use a little or a lot, depending on the garment, how much time and effort you want to spend, and the final effect you want to achieve. When you piece fabrics, it doesn't make much difference whether you do it by hand or machine because the seam is hidden. This is not true of appliqué. The technique you use, whether hand or machine, is obvious; it affects the final result, and it also affects the fabric—or vice versa. Sometimes the fabric dictates the method you'll use. Appliqué is a very personal and expressive art and as such offers endless opportunities for creativity. It has a fascinating history, and we are fortunate to have this tradition as a basis for our own exploration. In quiltmaking, almost all appliqué is done by hand; when you make a garment, you have a choice of hand or machine stitching. Whether you piece, appliqué, or use a mixture of the two, you also have to be thinking of a quilting pattern that will look right; you need not make a final decision when you begin, but the question should at least be tucked away in the back of your mind from the very start.

DESIGN SOURCES FOR APPLIQUÉ

You can use any kind of design you like on a garment. It can be curvy or flowing, stark or dramatic; details too small for appliqué can be brought out with either hand or machine embroidery. You may want just a touch of appliqué on the collar, cuffs, pocket, or belt of a dress or robe; you may want an appliqué design on the front of a skirt or the entire length of the hem. You can use just a little of it on a jacket, coat, or cape, or you can use it extravagantly. If you plan to cover most of a garment with appliqué, you won't need to be quite so fussy about the ground or basic fabric because most of it probably will not show. If you use separate appliqué designs, you must think of it from a positive–negative approach; the ground fabric of the shell is just as important as the fabric for the appliqué. You can work out details of the quilting design later, when the appliqué is complete.

14a. *"Rapunzel," designed and made by the author. The jacket is a square-cut pattern of unbleached muslin, machine quilted with polyester batt. Rapunzel is machine appliquéd to the shoulder, sleeve, and front of the jacket. The arm from the elbow down is separately finished and stuffed with quilt batting and attached at the elbow. Rapunzel's hand holds the jacket closed with a snap concealed in the palm.*

14b. *Back view of "Rapunzel" shows a friend watching eagerly as Rapunzel lets down her hair. A narrow band on the left sleeve covers the seam joining the sleeve to the jacket body.*

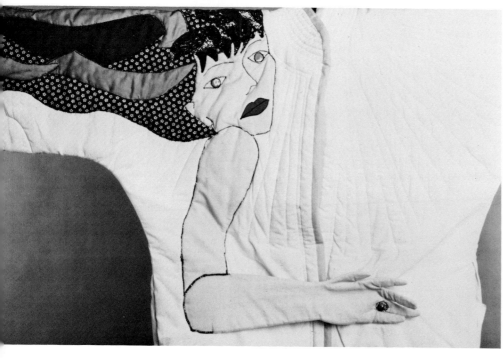

14c. *Detail of "Rapunzel" showing quilting lines fanned out from the neck.*

The first place to look for designs is the file of quilt patterns. The appliquéd quilt holds an exalted place in history, and it is inspiration enough just to look at some of the antique appliquéd quilts, or at least at photographs of them. Most of these patterns are formal or structured, but many of them have good designs that can easily be used in another context. Some of them may be too small for garment use because they are designed for quilt blocks, but remember, they can easily be enlarged. Seventy-five percent of all the appliqué quilt patterns we have on record are floral, and of these the rose is the most popular motif, with the tulip running a close second. Fruit, trees, birds, animals, fish, shells, and stars are all shapes of nature and ready to adapt for our own designs.

Appliqué may also be scenic or pictorial, and we may get ideas from advertisements, photographs, paintings, and drawings. Libraries offer tremendous rewards for they are filled with books and magazines on design. Also, there is the admirable list of Dover books, which are inexpensive and packed with ideas.

Symmetrical, geometric designs are suitable for appliqué too. "Snowflake" or Hawaiian-type designs work as beautifully on garments as they do on quilts. Other examples of appliqué can also provide inspiration—beaded designs from Indian tribes, leather appliqués from Egypt and Africa, the simple bold shapes of Colombian appliqués, the intricate work of molas or the ribbon appliqué from American Indians, or the scrolled and interwoven Celtic designs. We also get ideas from brush artists; Matisse, Calder, Miró, and Frank Stella have produced stunning works that could be adapted in many ways to fabric.

Plan your appliqué design as you planned your pieced design. Do you want shapes strategically placed or sewed to give an all-over effect? Try making this decision early, for it will help in planning garment design.

Almost any fabric can be used for appliqué—if you can get a needle through it. If you can't hand sew it, chances are it can be stitched with the machine. Appliqué fabrics should offer contrast to the ground fabric of your garment, either in texture or color. What we once thought of as unlikely combinations aren't unlikely at all by today's standards; we mix satin and wool, satin and velvet, satin and cotton, satin and lace. We put cotton with wool and silk; we pair chiffon or organza with felt or flannel, taffeta or moire with linen. We use smooth against nubby, dull against sheen. We can use a pile or wale fabric with the nap going in different directions so that it looks like several different fabrics instead of one. We can also utilize scraps from our piecing, both strip and Seminole work. Appliqué shapes cut from them are vibrant and unexpected, and in this instance nothing goes to waste!

15a. *"Mexican Hot Pepper," by the author. A square-cut jacket of handwoven Mexican cotton and hand-appliquéd red satin and velveteen, machine quilted with black and red thread, with some double needle quilting. Heavy diagonal quilting lines are stitched with twin needles, using black and red thread.*

15b. *Back view of "Mexican Hot Pepper." The back is hand appliquéd with red and black vinyl, then machine quilted.*

16a. *Child's quilted coat of polished cotton, by Galina Stepinoff-Darguery. The coat is channel quilted and bound in dark red cotton. The head and tail of a goose are the closures in the front.*

16b. *Back view of child's coat, showing goose appliquéd to coat back, then quilted.*

As you well know, appliqué is cutting a design from one or more fabrics and sewing these to a ground fabric—in this case, the ground fabric being the body of your garment. Appliqué shapes can be applied separately, or shapes can overlap and pile up on one another. They can be stuffed lightly, and they also can be faced and detached—that is, the appliqué can be sewed or tacked in one area to the garment and the rest of the shape hangs free. Sometimes, instead of creating your own design, you can cut one ready-made from printed fabrics. This is really the same technique used ages ago, called *broderie perse;* motifs were cut from English chintzes or Indian palimpores and sewed to a background of homespun. The motifs were floral, with exotic blooms and lush foliage, or preening birds with brilliant plumage, or other designs based on nature. With all the printed fabrics we have today, finding a suitable and special design should not present a problem.

Reverse appliqué can be used alone or combined with regular appliqué. Cut the design shape from the ground fabric for reverse appliqué, which, of course, leaves a hole there. Put the appliqué fabric of your choice underneath this hole so that there is a margin of a half-inch or more when the top fabric is sewed down. Do the stitching, then trim excess fabric from the underneath appliqué piece. You can also cut into this fabric and repeat the process of inserting another fabric underneath, then sewing it in place.

You can get lovely effects by covering appliqué fabric with a layer of organza or any other transparent fabric and sewing the sheer fabric when you sew the other. This creates a soft, misty effect.

We used to think that reverse appliqué had to be done with several layers of fabric stacked together. Starting at the top, we cut through successive layers to reveal color underneath. Of course we don't have to do that at all. You can cut directly into your ground fabric and sew the edges down to a piece of material just slightly larger than the cut you've made. You can do this repeatedly, and the nice thing is that you end up with the equivalent of one layer of fabric, with no unnecessary bulk, which makes reverse appliqué excellent for quilted items.

Either hand or machine stitching can be used for any type of appliqué. Both methods create entirely different effects, and you should consider this choice as an element of your design. Whenever you make a garment you are freed from many of the disciplines or rules you had to observe when making a quilt. For instance, you don't *have* to turn under the seam allowances of raw edges of an appliqué shape unless you want to. Sometimes raw edges left exposed add to textural interest; other materials, such as felt, leathers, suedes, some vinyls, and Ultrasuede fabric, do not have to have edges turned under since none of them fray or ravel when cut. And, while we're speaking of "special" fabrics, it is easier to appliqué a pieced design than to seam sections together. A Seminole design, for instance, would not be stitched, cut, and restitched in the traditional manner. You decide on the design you want, and, using a ruler and graph paper, draw a finished version of it. Make a cardboard template of the shapes involved—a square, a rectangle or a triangle, and so on, then cut these shapes from the material you are using. I did this working with Ultrasuede fabric. I had a three-color Seminole design and made templates for each shape, then cut them from the different colors using an X-Acto knife (or a Swann-Morton knife and blade). You must be accurate, however, for these shapes all butt up to each other to create the intended design. Work on a flat surface; I used a drop of rubber cement to hold the little squares and triangles in place until I could stitch them; a glue stick would serve the same purpose. I used the machine and top-stitched each shape very close to its outside edge. The whole design was far easier to handle this way than it would have been to seam strips of Ultrasuede fabric together and do it in the traditional way, and it looked fine.

STEPS FOR APPLIQUÉ

Remember what I said about there being no right way to do things. If it works for you, it's right. Without knowing any better many of us have sewed or pieced or appliquéd or quilted when the odds were against us. We have probably invented a lot of shortcuts and "things worth knowing." Any

17. *"Tulip" vest, by Pat Brousil. The hand-appliquéd design was adapted from a gardening book. Background is hand quilted with lines a quarter-inch apart.*

Fig. 10. *Enlarging a design with grids. Design may be enlarged to fill entire pattern space.*

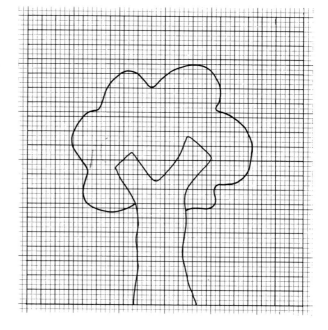

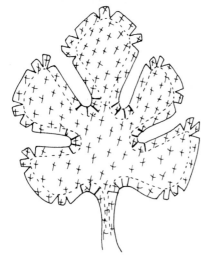

Fig. 10a. *Appliqué shape showing outside curves notched, inside curves clipped. Seam allowance is turned under along dotted line.*

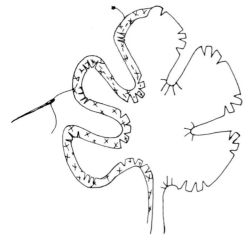

Fig. 10b. *Wrong side of appliqué shape, showing notches and clips, and seam allowance partly turned and basted.*

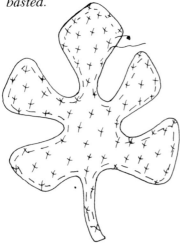

Fig. 10c. *Right side of appliqué design ready for placement and sewing to background fabric.*

appliquéing tips I have I want to pass on to you. Here are a few:

1. You don't always have to appliqué directly to the shell of your garment. You can appliqué to net or organdy, cut out around the completed design, leaving a turn-under, then appliqué it as a unit. This may help in many ways. If there is a lot of beading or sequin work on your design, you may not want to send it to the cleaners; beads can be damaged, and sequins sometimes melt. Simply clip the stitching, remove the appliqué, and when the garment comes back from the cleaners sew the piece back in place. You can mark the location with thread basting if that will help you.

2. You don't have to have full layers of fabric for reverse appliqué. You can cut the shape from the top layer or garment shell. Place the appliqué fabric underneath this, and sew the two layers together. You now look down or into this fabric, and it needs only to be large enough to cover the cut-out by a half-inch or so. If you like, you can also cut into this second layer, put a third fabric under it and repeat the process.

3. Some fabrics may not have enough sizing or body to hold their shape as appliqués. These can be backed with a second layer of the same fabric or a thin layer of batiste or other cotton. Often spray starch will add enough body to make sewing easy.

4. Turning under seam allowances for a neat finish can sometimes be a problem. With many cottons it is better to press the seam allowance over a cardboard template cut to finished size.

   Stay-stitch sharp points, deep angles, and deep curves before you cut the shape out. Draw the line of the design on fabric—and this is the finished line, not the cutting line—then machine stitch right next to it before you cut. This line of stitching makes it easier for you to turn under the seam allowance and keep it under control until you get it sewed down. This applies to hand work, of course, for most of the time you don't need to turn under the raw edge at all when you are using the machine for appliqué. You can turn it under, but you don't need to.

5. Clip curves if necessary to keep fabric from puckering.

6. Use a touch of fabric glue to hold an appliqué in place for sewing. You can also use Stitch-Witchery, following the instructions that come with it, but it is expensive. Or you can thread baste—an inexpensive and secure answer to this little problem.

7. Here's a tip for making bias strips, which can be used as flower stems or trailing vines or can cover the raw edges

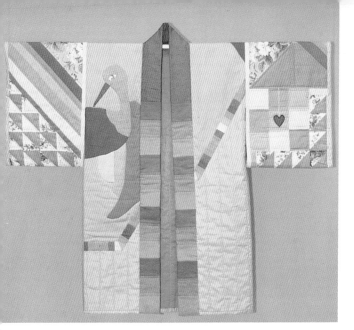

Plate 25. *Front view of Two Cranes coat, by Yvonne Porcella, Japanese haori coat (Porcella pattern), pieced, appliquéd, then quilted. Photo by Elaine F. Keenan.*

Plate 26. *Back view of Two Cranes coat. Photo by Elaine F. Keenan.*

Plate 27. *All silk pieced and quilted haori coat, by Yvonne Porcella. Sleeves button to coat body with tiny red buttons and loops. The coat can be worn sleeveless, and the sleeves can also be reversed. Author's collection.*

Plate 28. *A World Beyond the Clouds, a silk strip-patchwork and quilted coat, by Yvonne Porcella. Note ties on sleeves and sides. Coat is designed to hang flat on wall when not being worn. Photo by Elaine F. Keenan.*

Plate 29. *Bedding in Kimono Form, by Yvonne Porcella, back view. Photo by Elaine F. Keenan.*

Plate 30. *Back view of satin vest, by Janet Higgins. Machine quilted with silk thread, stitched through paper from the lining side.*

Plate 31. *Kandinsky Tabard, by Janet Higgins. Red satin vest quilted with silk and metallic thread, embellished with satin and velvet ribbons, sequins, and French knots.*

Plate 32. *Long Turkish-style robe, by Leslie English. Fabrics are Indian cotton, silk, and velvet, appliquéd and quilted, with a bright silk lining. Robe features horsehoof cuffs, vestiges of traditional Manchu riding costumes intended to cover the rider's hands.*

Plate 33. *Purple velvet jacket, by Leslie English, is quilted, with Persian antique gold brocade appliqués. Cuffs are handwoven of gold, indigo, and brown; the body of the coat is lined with orange Thai silk, and the sleeves with Paisley wool.*

Plate 34. *Orange silk vest, by Leslie English, is quilted and embellished with silk embroidery and silver beads. The vest is lined with a combination of three silk fabrics.*

Plate 35. *Front-view detail of a coat, designed by Jessica Joern, made of hand-painted silk, quilted, and lined in silk.*

Plate 36. *Front view of St. George and the Dragon vest, by Betty Mason. Appliquéd and quilted. Dragon scales are detached and machine satin-stitched the outside edges and extend over vest back.*

Plate 37. *Rainbow and Roses vest, by Betty Mason. Appliquéd and quilted in white with a machine zigzag stitch.*

Plate 38. *"Samurai" vest, by Jo Ann Giordano, idea based on Japanese Samurai armor. Acetate, rayon and resist-dyed cotton are pieced and machine quilted. (See also Photo 11 for back view.)*

Plate 39. *Cosmic Fantasy jacket, by Jo Ann Giordano. Chinese-style quilted jacket of silk pongee, hand screened with pattern of oscilloscope and atomic particle lines.*

Plate 40. *Tibetan panel coat, by Sherry Schmauder. All-cotton fabric, with strip piecing in alternate panels. Panels are lined, stitched, and turned, then joined with decorative machine stitches. Seminole piecing on shoulder flanges. Filler used only in front band, then hand quilted. No filler in body of garment. Porcella pattern.*

Plate 41. *Front view of "Arabic Jacket #1," by Sonya Barrington. All cotton, machine pieced, and hand quilted.*

Plate 42. *Harlequin Jacket, in twenty-one shades of velveteen, stripped with curved seam piecing, by Michael James. Design in random geometric arrangement, built on horizontal rows in graduated widths crossed by diagonal seams. Funnel neck jacket, closed with loops and buttons, using double thickness traditional polyester batting. Assembled and sewn by Judy James.*

Plate 43. *Mariner's Compass cape, by Lesly-Claire Greenberg. Pieced from eighty different cotton prints and several shades of Ultrasuede fabric. String-quilted yoke with collar of jesters' points with bells.*

Plate 44. *Jacket, pieced, quilted, and appliquéd, by Joanne Stark. Calicos, batiks, and other fabrics were strip-pieced and quilted to the base fabric. Ribbons and trims cover raw edges. Feathered tail of bird was appliquéd over piecing, and edges were couched with heavy yarn.*

Plate 45. *Quilted cotton coat, by Diana Leone. Log cabin pattern uses reds and blues instead of traditional light and dark.*

Plate 46. *Kimono #2, by Jacqueline Snyders Halinski. Silk, cotton, and other fabrics were pieced, appliquéd, and quilted, with dramatic use of trapunto quilting. Kimono may be hung on wall when not being worn.*

Plate 47. *Detail of Kimono #2.*

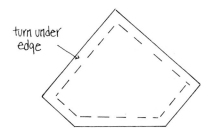
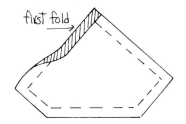
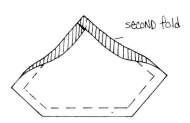

Fig. 11a. *Sewing a right-angle point by two-fold method.*

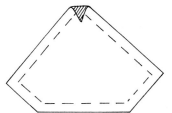
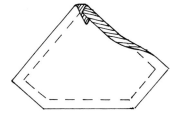
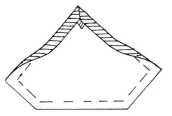

Fig. 11b. *Sewing a right-angle point by three-fold method.*

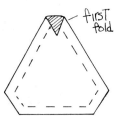
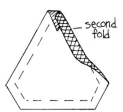
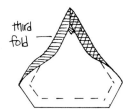

Fig. 11c. *Sewing an acute-angle point by three-fold method.*

of seams. They can also be used for intricate scrolled appliqué designs, such as the Celtic ones. Since they are bias they will follow any line you give them. A little book published a couple of years ago titled *Celtic Quilt Designs* gives what are basically traditional designs adapted for quiltmaking by Philomena Wiechec. She developed a method for making bias strips that should assure her of a place in the needlecrafters' hall of fame. Always before, I had stitched bias to make a tube, then spent time, disposition, and temper trying to turn this tube right side out in any of a dozen ways, none of which were foolproof. Philomena came up with a dandy remedy: don't turn the tube. And she's right. She also came up with another good idea; she developed thin metal strips, one a half-inch (12 mm) wide, another a quarter-inch (6 mm) wide, both twelve inches (30 cm) long and with rounded ends. You slip the metal strip inside a fold of true bias, wrong side of fabric inside. With

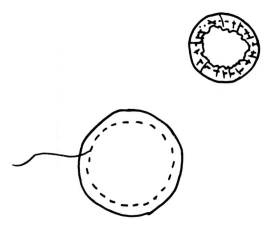

Fig. 12. *Sewing circles. Cut circle larger than desired size. With a single thread sew running stitches around outer edge of circle; pull up on stitches, turning raw edge to inside. Circle can be stuffed lightly if desired. Sew folded edge of circle to ground fabric with blind stitches.*

the zipper foot on your machine, stitch through the folded fabric next to the metal strip. When you near the end of the strip, slide it further down in the fabric fold and keep on stitching until you have the required length. Now, trim the seam allowance to one-eighth inch (3 mm) or less, and with your fingers move the seam over until it lies in the middle of the strip rather than to the side. Leave until you've pressed, then remove it. The tube, whatever its width, is now ready to use; you can apply it by hand to create a design or cover seams, or you can top-stitch both edges with the machine. These bias strips can also be used for floral stems or as the "leading" in stained-glass fabric patterns. If you don't have, or can't find, the metal strips, don't despair. Cut strips from cardboard; they work very well, and you can cut any width you like.

Sewing a bias tube in this manner is far easier than cutting a bias strip, then basting and pressing under the required seam allowances before stitching it in place.

HAND STITCHES FOR APPLIQUÉ

The stitches most commonly used for hand appliqué are explained in depth in *The Big Book of Appliqué,* but I'll refresh your memory.

You can use a blind or slip stitch, or a whipping or hemming stitch, using matching thread. Keep your stitches even, close together, and as tiny as possible. You can hold the folded edge toward you or away from you, whichever is easier.

You can also use a running stitch, or a feather, herringbone, buttonhole, blanket, or chain stitch, with floss instead of thread, or perle cotton or crochet cotton, buttonhole twist, yarn, or metallic thread. It all depends on the effect you want. Whatever you use, be sure the appliqué is secured to the shell of the garment; you don't want it to slip or go slithering off if you chance to lean back against a chair.

MACHINE APPLIQUÉ

Most of you have sewing machines or at least are planning to get one. Most of you also have used the machine to make clothes for yourself or for the kids, to make draperies or bedspreads or slipcovers, and maybe you've used it to mend too. You may not realize what a treasure you have; next to my piano, I love my sewing machines. A machine not only stitches seams but finishes them; it can give you dozens of fancy stitches, a decorative ballet; it can make buttonholes,

18a. *Walking suit, by Della Collins, with rooster appliqué and quilted jacket.*

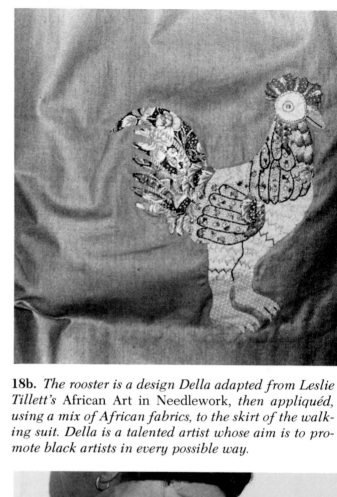

18b. *The rooster is a design Della adapted from Leslie Tillett's* African Art in Needlework, *then appliquéd, using a mix of African fabrics, to the skirt of the walking suit. Della is a talented artist whose aim is to promote black artists in every possible way.*

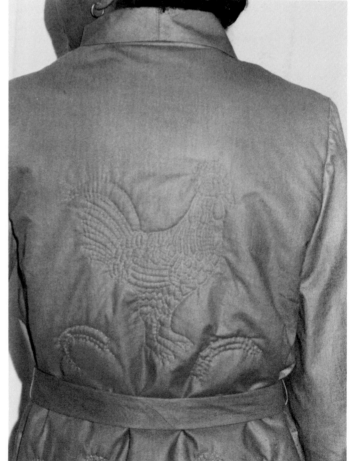

18c. *Back view of walking suit jacket shows how the appliquéd rooster has been used as a quilting pattern to emphasize design and add unity to the outfit.*

Fig. 13. *Square-cut garment showing all-over appliqué design.*

draw, and embroider. It can also stitch with two or even three needles to give you close parallel lines in the easiest, most professional way. If you keep your machine clean and oiled, it does all of these things without complaint, performing tirelessly for you. Machine appliqué often involves more than straight stitching, but whether you use straight or zig-zag stitching, try a few test runs first.

Once you've decided on the placement of your design, be sure the appliqué is held securely to the garment section. If the design pieces are small, a spot of glue stick will help hold them. If they are large shapes, you might want to use both glue stick and thread basting. I seldom pin baste; the pins fall out, and there is always the danger of hitting one with a needle, snagging the fabric, or breaking the needle. I do use pins to help stitch difficult areas, but I am careful to pull them out as I come to them.

If you thread baste, you can use either hand basting or machine basting. I use hand basting inside a large shape because it is much easier to remove; sometimes I machine baste around the outside edge of an appliqué shape since it will be covered later with a finishing stitch. Also, well-basted work makes stitching easier; both hands are free to guide the fabric under the presser foot to make sure that it doesn't bunch up. If you straight stitch or top-stitch your appliqué in place, it is easier to turn under the raw edges ahead of time, even press them, before you do the stitching. If you plan to use a satin stitch or closed zigzag (certainly the most popular stitch), then you don't need to turn under the seam allowance because the stitching will cover the raw edge.

The trick with any of this is to keep the work from puckering, and if the appliqué has any appreciable size, it will help to baste it first. I usually machine baste with a narrow, open zigzag stitch. This holds the work in place, and the basting stitch will be covered with the final satin stitch, so there is no need to remove it.

Your choice of fabric dictates the thread you should use, and the thread, in turn, dictates the size of the needle. I have found, however, that machine embroidery thread works very well in a satin stitch on most fabrics; it seems to keep the stitches from piling up on top of each other. Before

Fig. 15. *Folding paper to cut a pattern, Hawaiian style. First fold is horizontal; paper is folded again to make a square; folded edges are then brought together to make a triangle.*

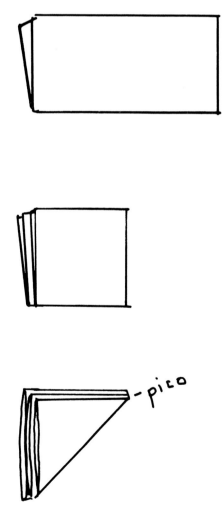

Fig. 14. *Square-cut garment with Hawaiian-type design. Dotted lines show echo quilting lines.*

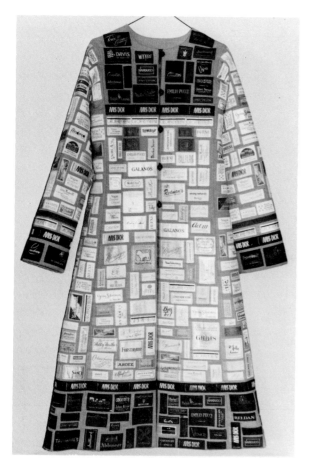

19b. *Detail of the "Label Coat." Labels were machine stitched to wool coating and batting, then hand quilted with black thread around each one.*

19a. *"Label Coat," designed and made by Shirley Fomby. Shirley used 642 labels in her coat, collected from friends and a few designers. These were laid out, puzzle fashion, on beige wool, with the white background labels on the body of the coat and the black background labels on the yoke, sleeves, and hem.*

19c. *Another detail of the "Label Coat." The 642 labels came from 48 people and represent 16 states and 18 countries.*

you start stitching, pull out three or four inches (7–10 cm) of thread both from the bobbin and needle, and hold them in back of the work. Put the needle in starting position, lower the presser foot, and hold on to those threads until you've taken the first few stitches and things are running smoothly. When you come to a corner, make sure that the needle is on the outside, or at the farthest point of a right-hand swing. When the stitching is finished, cut the thread, again leaving enough so that you can pull the top thread to the wrong side and tie it.

Another way to finish the edges of appliqué after you've machine basted is to couch yarn or cord around the outside edge. Set the zigzag stitch so that it will swing over the cord and into the fabric on both sides, and keep the stitch open so that the cord will show through. You can use either matching or contrasting thread for this.

We all know what strip quilting is. It eliminates one step, combines piecing and quilting, and is used primarily for a reversible garment. In a similar manner, you can appliqué and quilt at the same time by stitching your appliqué through the fabric shell as well as a layer of batting. I don't suggest you appliqué-quilt through the lining too, for the result is never quite as professional as it should be. Before you try this—or any quilting—on your machine, loosen the pressure. The pressure screw or wheel regulates the space between the presser foot and the bed of the machine, and you need a little more space when you are stitching through bulky layers. Frankly I think in the long run it is easier and looks better to appliqué first and save the quilting for later.

Stabilizing often helps in machine appliqué. Two or three layers of fabric, especially those of different weight

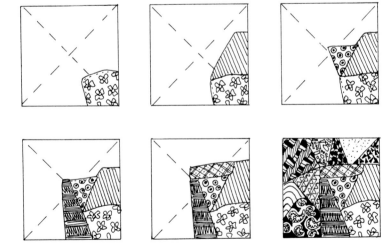

Fig. 16. *Steps in constructing a crazy-patch quilt block. The first piece of fabric is basted in place on a foundation of fabric or paper; the second piece overlaps it and is sewed down; the third overlaps the second, and so on. The same construction techniques can easily be used for garments. Cut foundation to pattern shape, then cover as instructed above.*

and texture, won't always go through the machine at the same speed, and when this happens you have puckers—sometimes lots of them. An even-feed or walking-foot attachment for your machine often helps a great deal, not only in appliqué but later on in quilting. You can also slip tissue paper, tracing paper, or blank newsprint under the work, stitch through it, and tear the paper away later. There is also a product on the market called Tear-away, which is made specifically as a stabilizer for machine appliqué. It works very well, and, as the name promises, it tears away when the stitching is finished.

Some "special" fabrics require special techniques when you sew with them, and the stabilizers, paper or Tear-away, and even-feed or walking-foot attachments are unquestionably a help. I have three sewing machines, two of which I use all the time—but for different jobs. Each has a distinct personality, and they do everything but talk back to me. There are times when I think they do that too. One of them, for instance, doesn't like to sew on Ultrasuede fabric or even real leathers. The machine skips stitches—deliberately, I'm convinced—and not just a few but sometimes a whole row. The Skinner Company, which manufactures Ultrasuede fabric, has a little instruction book all about sewing on it, and although I read and followed the instructions to the letter, I had nothing but rebellion and disaster at hand. I had quite the opposite experience with the other machine; it *loves* Ultrasuede fabric and merrily stitches right along with a happy rhythm. I do use paper as a stabilizer, but I don't need to use the walking-foot; this machine will piece, appliqué, and quilt this elegant fabric without hesitation. But, determined to put down the rebellion from this first machine, I tried several different approaches; the first was a change of needles. The all-purpose yellow-band needle made by Singer Company was one persuasion; the other was using paper as a stabilizer, and I have had no trouble since.

Coated fabrics occasionally have to be coddled too. These fabrics can be porous or nonporous and are produced mainly for rainwear. The needle sticks in these fabrics, which makes stitching difficult, but I find if I "paint" the stitching line just ahead of the needle with a Q-tip dipped lightly in sewing machine oil, I don't have a problem. The oil wipes away easily.

Ciré and nylon are both popular for cold-weather wear. Either of these can be pieced, appliquéd, or just quilted, but a new, sharp needle is a must.

I haven't met your sewing machine, but if there is a strained relationship between it and the fabrics you want to stitch, praise it, speak warmly to it, try a few new approaches in technique, and everything will work out.

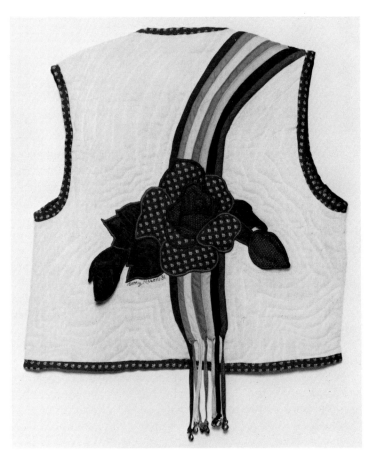

20. *"Rainbow and Roses" vest, by Betty Mason. The rose is detached machine appliqué, using fine satin stitch around the edges. Batting, quilting, and satin-stitched details give body to the flower. The rainbow ends in a fringe. The vest is contour hand quilted.*

21. *Velvet vest, by Bonnie Case. Appliqués are cut from chintz and metallic fabrics; sequins, beads, and embroidery are added for embellishment. Cord is couched around the sleeve area and down the front of the vest.*

6

ADDED ATTRACTIONS AND SHORT SUBJECTS

Embellishment is that little extra something that sets a garment apart, establishing it without doubt as unique, with individual touches that cannot be duplicated. Embellishment not only adds interest but, more often, whimsy, surprise, and wonder. As a quilter, stitcher, and sewer, you have a collection, I'm sure, of "odds and ends" that you have tucked away over the years. I have tucked mine in clear plastic shoe boxes so I can see what goodies lie within; I am stunned occasionally to realize that these shoe boxes fill two shelves in my workroom, stacked two deep, and that there are still a few in the attic. I keep everything, with the inborn conviction that sooner or later I'll be able to use it.

Embellishment as such can't be confined to a cut and dried list—remember E. B. White's "One Man's Meat Is Another Man's Poison"? I have buttons—plastic, glass, ceramic, cork, and crocheted. I have shells, but only the kind with a tiny hole punched in them so that you can attach them easily. I have all kinds of beads, fake pearls, old costume jewelry, seed necklaces, and wood and cork beads. I have sequins, shi-sha mirrors in assorted sizes, tassels, feathers, plastic and fabric tubing, artificial flowers and leaves, bits of ribbons, and interesting pieces of embroidery, crochet, and lace. I also have a few antique "medals" with silk ribbons attached—not really medals, but they look like them. They say "Guest," or "Lodge No. 816," or something like that, and the year is printed in gilt numbers. I have one such ribbon I often pin to whatever I'm wearing; it says "Grand Bodies."

Most or all of these gadgets can be used at one time or another if you feel like it. They can be sewed down fast or left to dangle. You can couch tubing or cord or even light chain, and you can add lace or crocheted doilies or bits of ribbon too pretty to throw away. I made yo-yos—those little gathered circles of fabric so in vogue years and years ago—and attached them to one sleeve of my coat "Lightning Strikes Twice" (*Plates 64, 65*), and from the center of each I hung one of my saved treasures to dangle as I walk. Braids often add an elegant touch to a garment, and tassels create equal interest.

Embellishment is not confined to the body of a garment. There are many ways you can emphasize seams to give them a whole new look. Welting, piping, ruffles, pleats,

74

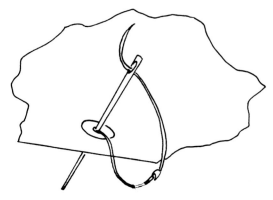

Fig. 17a. *An individual sequin sewed and held in place with a bead.*

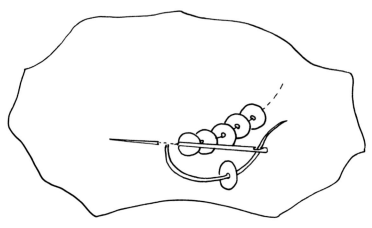

Fig. 17b. *Sequins sewed in a row.*

prairie points, and bindings are just a few of the alternatives to consider, and you should add fringe to this list.

PIPING AND WELTING

Piping and welting differ only in size. Welting is seen most often on the seams of slipcovers and upholstery, but there isn't any reason why you can't use it in a garment if you want something of that size. Piping is available ready-made in many shops, but often it doesn't match or the fabric isn't

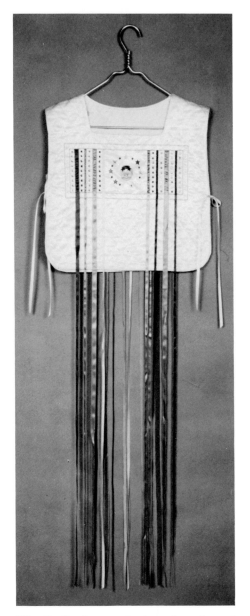

22. *Quilted vest, designed and made by Janet Higgins. It is of white satin, cut tabard-style with ties at side. Satin ribbons stream from front and back, and sewed to the front is a porcelain face by Sherrie Zeitkin.*

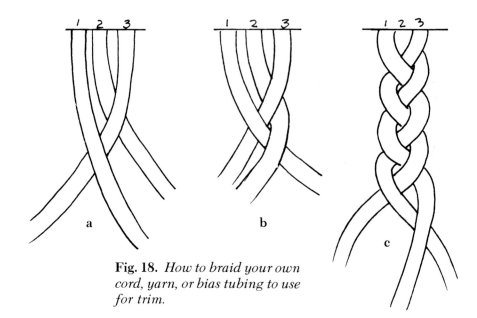

Fig. 18. *How to braid your own cord, yarn, or bias tubing to use for trim.*

top quality, and you are better off making your own. Use narrow cord or butcher's string, and cut true bias strips wide enough to encase the cord and to leave one-quarter to three-eighths of an inch (6–10 mm) for a seam allowance. You may need to piece your bias strips to get the required length, and remember to piece on straight grain and then press these little seams open. Fold the bias strip with the right side of fabric outside and the cord inside, then pin at frequent intervals; this will keep the bias from stretching as you sew. Now, with a zipper foot on the machine, stitch or baste through both layers of fabric close to the cord. When you use this piping in a seam, don't try to do everything in one operation; it simply doesn't work. Machine or hand baste the piping in place first. When you are ready for the final stitching, stitch from the side of the basted piping. The line of basting stitches is a guide, and you can stitch one thread or so inside it, next to the cord, for a very professional finished look. Use this same method in attaching ruffles, pleating, fringe, and sometimes, prairie points.

RUFFLES

Ruffles can be cut on the straight or the bias grain, and they may be single or double and as full or skimpy as you like. Double ruffles eliminate the need for finishing the outside edge, although some ruffles can be used with raw edges, especially if they are cut on the bias. These ruffles can be stitched *into* the seams, or they can be top-stitched to the

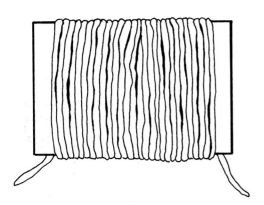

Fig. 19a. *Make your own tassels by first winding yarn over cardboard.*

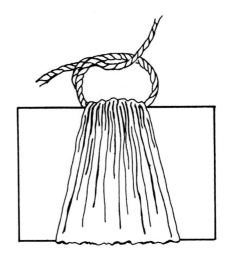

Fig. 19b. *Slip yarn underneath the strands before removing tassel from cardboard; tie to secure, either at top or underneath yarns (Fig. 19c) to conceal the ends.*

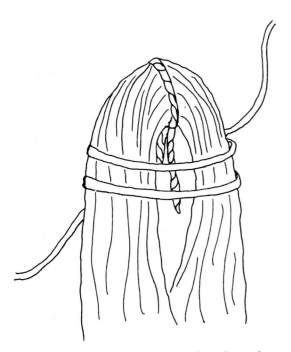

Fig. 19c. *Tassel is wrapped with cord or yarn below top section.*

Fig. 19d. *Tassel ready to use.*

outside of the garment with ribbon or tape covering the gathered raw edges. Pleated ruffles can be used effectively too; either of these can be slipped under a decorative pleat in your garment and then top-stitched in place. A two-to-one ratio is good to use in making your own ruffles. Cut fabric length twice as long as the finished ruffle, use two lines of machine basting for the gathers, and pull up on the bob-

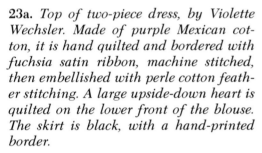

23a. *Top of two-piece dress, by Violette Wechsler. Made of purple Mexican cotton, it is hand quilted and bordered with fuchsia satin ribbon, machine stitched, then embellished with perle cotton feather stitching. A large upside-down heart is quilted on the lower front of the blouse. The skirt is black, with a hand-printed border.*

24. *Jacket detail of garment by Chita Becker. The roundel shows quilting and embroidery against a background of channel quilting. See complete jacket on page 83.*

23b. *Detail of Violette Wechsler's blouse, showing hand quilting.*

bin threads. Many machines also have a pleating or ruffling attachment; if you have one, use it. We've been brainwashed to think that ruffles should go around a neck or the bottom of a sleeve, but this is no longer true. Use them vertically as well as horizontally and in any seam, tuck, or pleat your garment may have.

PRAIRIE POINTS

Prairie points are triangles. I don't know where they got their name, but they've been around for a long time. Many an old-time quiltmaker (and now, many new quiltmakers) edged quilts with prairie points. They create an interesting sawtooth edge and are equally effective in garments, in seams, in tucks or pleats, with braid or ribbon holding them in place, or around necklines and hems. There are two "real" ways to make them and a third I devised, which I call a mock prairie point. Any of these can be any size; and they can be used singly or in a row. A square of fabric is the basis for all of them.

For prairie point method no. 1, fold the square on the diagonal. You now have a triangle. Fold again on the diagonal to make a smaller triangle. Where the first bias folds come together there will be an opening. Pin this triangle across the cotton raw edge to keep it from unfolding. Now make a second triangle in the same way, and, keeping the bias fold opening to your right, slip the other side of the triangle barely inside the opening of the first triangle so that the bottom edges overlap. Repeat as many times as you want, pinning or basting along the bottom edges.

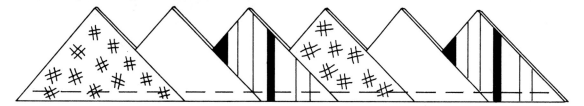

Fig. 20. *Prairie point method no. 1, with fabric square folded on diagonal, then folded a second time on diagonal. Start with two of these, then slip folded side of second triangle into folded open side of first triangle; continue until you have enough.*

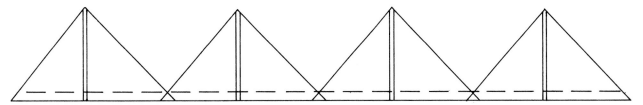

Fig. 21. *Prairie point method no. 2. Fabric square is folded horizontally. Mark the midpoint of the fold. Bring each side of folded edge to the middle, then to right angles to bottom raw edge. The prairie point opening is now in the middle of the triangle instead of the side. These triangles are joined with the edges meeting, not overlapping.*

For prairie point method no. 2, fold the fabric square in half horizontally instead of diagonally. This makes a rectangle. Mark the midpoint of the folded edge, then bring both halves of this edge down at right angles to the bottom. This leaves a little folded opening in the middle of the triangle rather than at the side. Also, when you use more than one in a seam or at the edge, you do not overlap them; the bottom edge of one just meets the bottom edge of the next. You can use prairie points no. 2 as closures also. Make a vertical machine buttonhole in the center of the horizontally folded square, then complete the folding to form the finished triangle. Stitch the closures along the outside front edge of your garment.

My mock method (Prairie Point no. 2) requires sewing, but it goes very fast. Use two fabric squares, right sides together, and machine stitch at a quarter-inch all the way around. Now cut in half diagonally, then turn and press. This gives you a faced triangle instead of a folded one. Using two different fabrics or colors in stitching also gives you added variety.

Any kind of embroidery may be added to a garment. You can cover pieced seams or appliquéd edges with it, or you can quilt with it. You can also use it for couching or as an extension of lace or crocheted edges. One of the most interesting and unusual ways to use embroidery is in attaching shi-sha mirrors. These little bits of mica in varied and irregular shapes are used predominantly in India and Pakistan, but I'm happy to say we also use them here. Some shops sell little packages of mirrors, and you can substitute these for mica if you can't find the real thing. These little mirrors are

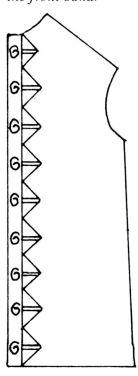

Fig. 22. *Front of garment showing prairie point method no. 2 stitched in the front band.*

Fig. 23. *Herringbone stitch. Use for embroidery, decorative seam finish, or as a quilting stitch. This is often called a "catch stitch" when used in sewing.*

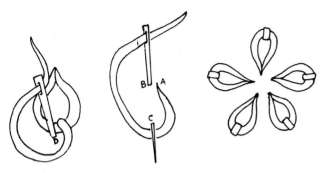

Figs. 24a and 24b. *Detached chain stitch or lazy daisy stitch.*

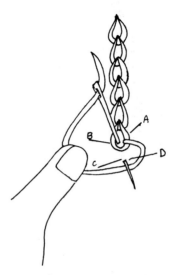

Fig. 24c. *Chain stitch worked from top to bottom. Use in embroidered accents or as a quilting stitch.*

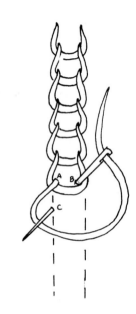

Fig. 24d. *Open chain stitch worked between two imaginary parallel lines. It may also be used as a quilting stitch or to couch cord or yarn.*

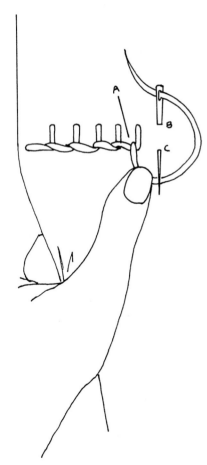

Fig. 25. *Buttonhole or blanket stitch. Buttonhole stitch is worked close together, a blanket stitch with some space in between.*

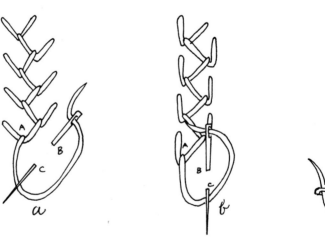

Fig. 26. *Feather stitch and variations, for use in embroidery or as a quilting stitch.*

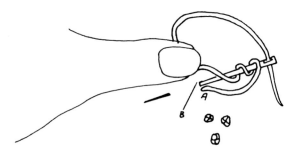

held to fabric with a network of embroidery stitches; first, you have to weave a foundation, with straight stitches crossing and criss-crossing the mirror so it won't slip. Then, using a cretan, buttonhole, or lazy daisy stitch, work into the foundation and the fabric not only to conceal the foundation but to add ornamentation to the mirror or mica. Other embroidery stitches may be used, but these are the most common. When the mica is secured, if you can't leave well enough alone, you can add French knots or other stitches to increase the circumference and add to the drama. (One source for shi-sha mirrors, in thirteen different sizes and shapes, is The World in Stitches, 82 South Street, Milford, New Hampshire 03055. Another is Kitsophrenia, Inc., Box 5042, Glendale, California 91201. In the United Kingdom you can buy them from Silk & Strand, 33 Linksway, Gateley, Cheshire.)

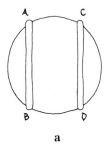

a

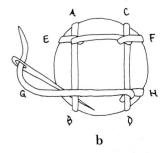

b

Fig. 28. *Figures a, b, and c show the working foundation stitches to attach shi-sha mirrors to fabric. When the foundation is finished, work cretan stitch closely all the way around, stitching from the outside edge of the mirror, through the fabric, and into the center of the foundation stitches (d). Pull stitches together snugly. Buttonhole stitch may also be used instead of cretan.*

c

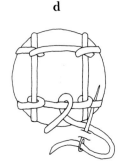

d

25a. *"Victoria," by Judy Murrah. This is a quilted collage vest of old needlework pieces and antique crochet and lace, some made by machine and some by hand. Vest fabrics are silk, satin, and velvet. The front yoke sections are cut from an old dresser scarf embroidered in silk.*

25b. *Back view of "Victoria." The back yoke, with cupids and flowers of antique crochet filet, was once part of a long table runner.*

Speaking of leaving well enough alone, don't get carried away and add everything all at once; pick and choose and save something for the next time. You want to add to your garment, not detract from it.

Embellishments and embroidery are certainly added attractions to a garment, but there is another type of added attraction we haven't mentioned except in passing. Those are the personal accessories—belts, body jewelry, boots, and other items—which in miniature or small quantities can be quilted too. These can be as simple or as elaborate as the garment. Often if you want to test out a design or idea you're not quite sure about, this is a good way to do it. A belt of twisted cord might have a quilted medallion in front; a wide, obi-shaped belt could be beaded, appliquéd, and quilt-

26. *Quilted jacket designed and made by Chita Becker. Pockets are decorated with quilted and embroidered roundels of roses and leaves.*

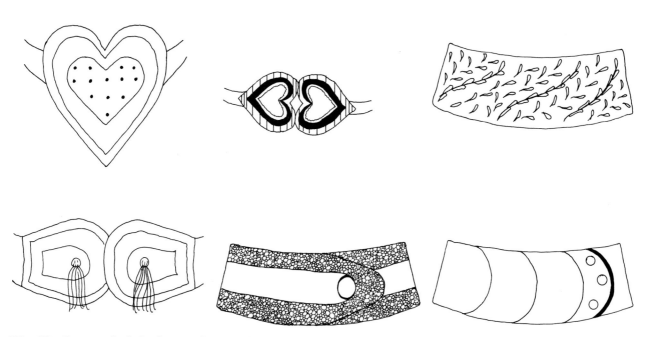

Fig. 29. *Six simple belt shapes that can be pieced, appliquéd, or embellished with embroidery or findings. They may be padded and then quilted by hand or machine or a combination of both.*

27a-f. *A series of quilted necklaces or body adornments by Marie Berler.*

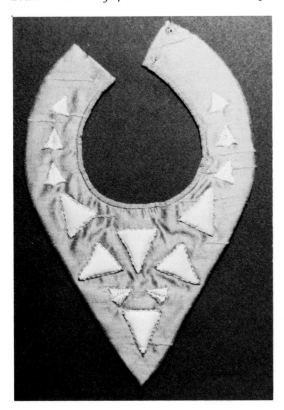

27a. *"Arrows" are made of satin, puffed appliqués padded with polyester batting, and surface embroidery.*

27b. *"Lei" consists of metallic brocade flowers that are stuffed, then appliquéd to a padded quilted necklace.*

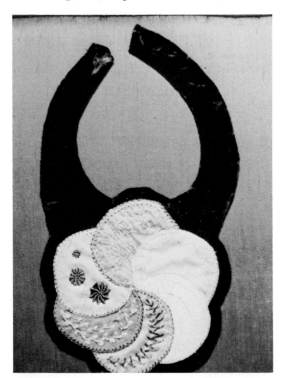

27c. *"Pinwheel" is made from embroidered satin circles appliquéd to a padded velvet neckpiece.*

ed to your heart's content. So can body jewelry, from a small pin worn on the shoulder or lapel to a complex bib-like creation that changes a simple dress to a drop-dead creation.

Such items are not only fun to make but are also a challenge and make wonderful gifts. They also take less time than a garment and offer a change of pace when you sandwich something small in between two bigger projects.

Aside from testing designs with these added attractions, you can also test techniques from fabric to filler, hand to machine, and perhaps save yourself time and effort later. All of these certainly do come under the heading of quilts to wear, as do hats—berets, caps, bonnets, cloches, brimmed hats, and hoods. Enough to keep you busy for a long long time.

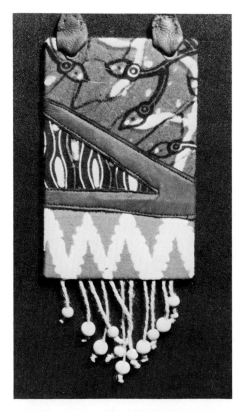

27d. *"Africa Thing"* consists of African tribal cottons and leather, machine stitched through batting, and ties with leather thongs.

27e. (Below left) *"Bali Thing"* is made of Indonesian cotton that is quilted. Fabric pendants are stuffed, pulled through bamboo slices, and attached to bib.

27f. (Below right) *"Shasta"* is a neckpiece of velvets and satins. Appliqués are stiffened with heavy Pellon, edged with a buttonhole stitch, and then attached to the necklace.

7

TRAPUNTO AND OTHER QUILTING

Once the shell of the garment is finished, it's time to think about quilting. No doubt you've already thought about it, as to style or design, and what your final decision will be depends on the garment. If you are making an all-quilted or "whole-cloth" garment, then, of course, the quilting design and technique have been of prime importance from the first. It's difficult to describe the aesthetic hold quilting has on us; sometimes people become almost inarticulate, trying to convey its importance. It takes longer than most other types of needlework, except perhaps for needlepoint, but it is also far more open to inspection and criticism—and praise—than its sister skills. Quilting adds new depth and dimension to design and fabric, it offers contrasts in light and shadow, and it creates a texture all its own. When used with piecing or appliqué, it often creates pattern on pattern, a visual delight, a feast for the eyes.

The two major forms of quilting are trapunto and traditional American. Trapunto is Italian in origin, as far as I know, and although it has been around for hundreds of years, only recently has it begun to come into its own in the United States. Originally it was very formal, very elegant, and it did not appear to be readily adaptable to Americans' casual way of living and dressing. After experimenting with it and using it in a variety of ways, we know now it can add appreciably to quilting techniques, whether used alone or in conjunction with traditional work.

Trapunto consists of two techniques, cording and stuffing, which can be used alone or together, depending on the effect you want in your work. You use two layers of fabric for trapunto, the outer, top, or shell fabric and a thin woven backing—batiste or voile. You can use a heavier backing fabric, unbleached muslin for instance, but often that decision depends on the top fabric, its weight and texture. These two layers are basted together and handled as a single fabric. The trapunto design is stitched through both layers. Double and usually parallel lines are stitched for cording, and a single line of stitching marks the stuffed areas. The channels for cording are as narrow or as wide as the cording or yarns to be threaded through them, and they can be either hand or machine stitched. You don't need to have a special pattern for trapunto work because almost any pattern or design can be adapted for it. Pare it to the essentials, or change it any way you like. Decide which parts of the pattern you

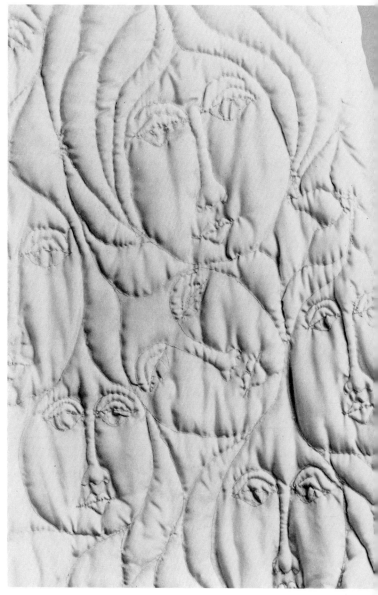

28a. *"Face Cape," by Elsa Brown. Off-white polyester crepe in a beautiful example of trapunto-stuffed quilting. The machine-stitched faces are lost in swirling seas of quilting.*

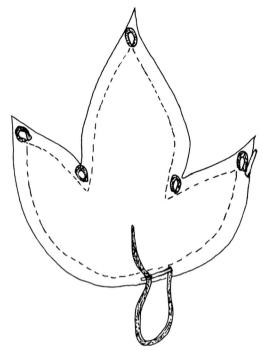

Fig. 30a. *Trapunto cording technique. Cord or yarn is threaded through a stitched channel with a tapestry needle, leaving a small loop of yarn at points, angles, and deep curves.*

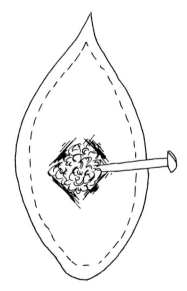

Fig. 30b. *Trapunto stuffing technique. Small bits of polyfil or other stuffing are poked through a slit or small hole in the backing fabric into the pocket made by stitching two layers of fabric together.*

want to cord and which to stuff, then do the stitching. Cording is often used to outline a design and perhaps emphasize detail; you can also use it to fill in areas completely with rows of stitching lined up side by side.

I mention trapunto now because, if you want to use it along with traditional or regular quilting, the trapunto must be done first, before any batting or filler is added. If you use it alone, then all you need to do is line the garment when the trapunto is finished and all the seams are sewed.

You can mark the design on the backing, then stitch from the backing, too, which eliminates any marking on the shell side. If you hand stitch, a tiny running stitch in matching or contrasting thread is best to use since the stitches look the same from either side. You also can machine stitch from the backing side. Use a fairly short stitch, and tie threads to secure them; do not lock stitch or back tack. If your design is centered or covers just a small area, trim away the excess backing fabric when the stitching is finished. If you have cut the backing the same size as the shell pattern pieces, leave it and catch it in the seams.

If the cording or yarn is thin enough, you can machine stitch the channels with a double needle from the shell side. This gives you lovely parallel lines an eighth of an inch (3 mm) apart with a minimum of effort. A size 16 or 18 tapestry needle (with a blunt end), threaded with the cord or yarn, is good to use for cording. You work from the back. Poke the needle into the backing at the end of the line, and try not to go through both layers. Then slide the needle along through the channel. Whenever you come to a deep

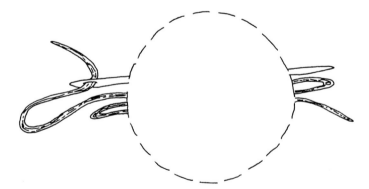

Fig. 30c. *Small areas, such as circles, too small to slit, may be stuffed with yarn strands. Start tapestry needle through the center area of the stitched-together fabrics and work out from each side. Yarn strands lie close together, filling the area.*

angle, sharp point or corner, or deep curve, you must bring the needle out of the backing fabric and check to see that the cord or yarn already inserted lies flat in its channel. Now, insert the needle into the same hole and begin to fill the next channel, leaving a tiny loop of yarn poking up from the hole. This little loop acts as insurance and will keep your work from puckering.

For different effects, try colored yarns or cords threaded through the channels, or try cords of varying sizes. Be sure the stitched channel is large enough to accommodate the cord, then work it through with a little safety pin or bodkin. The beginnings and ends of the cord or yarn do not need to be fastened down; just clip them about a half-inch (12 mm) from the fabric and leave them alone.

Trapunto stuffing is also done from the backing side. Cut a little slit in the backing of the area to be stuffed—and be more careful than ever that you don't cut through both layers of fabric! Use polyfil to stuff these areas, but poke in tiny bits at a time or else they ball up and stick together and refuse to cooperate at all. Stuff the outside parts near the stitching line and the corners first, and then work up to the slit you've cut. If you cut the slit on the bias instead of the straight grain, it won't fray so badly. Check the stuffed areas from the right side to be sure they are even, then close up the hole. Lace a few stitches across the slit, and don't try to pull the edges together. I've tried all kinds of "stuffing" tools—Q-tip, crochet hook, knitting needle, orangewood stick, toothpick, and even the end of my sharp little scissors. I'll leave that to you; stuff with any tool that works well for you.

Occasionally I work from the outer or top side rather than the backing. If I am machine stitching, I draw the design on tracing paper, stitch through it, and tear the paper off when I'm finished. If I am working by hand, I use a hard lead or charcoal pencil.

Elsa Brown, a fabric artist from Connecticut, works almost wholly with trapunto and with white or off-white fabrics. She does all her machine stitching with a darning foot because it enables her to go in any direction and put in details that otherwise might be difficult. She uses faces, heads, and people as major elements in her designs, and her book *Creative Quilting* shows quite a variety of them. Her "Moth Jacket" is one of her newer pieces. It is a cropped jacket of polyester satin and looks wonderfully light and fluffy. Elsa also has achieved marvelous effects by using dark backing fabrics—black, navy, gray, or brown—with the white or off-white top. The combination creates interesting shadows around the stitching lines and adds an exciting dimension to the design. She seldom uses cording but concentrates her technique on stuffing.

29. *Trapunto butterfly adorns the front of a polyester satin gown, designed and made by Elsa Brown.*

30. *"Morning Mist" in progress, designed and made by the author. The photo shows the lining side of hand-quilted gray cotton. Front and back sections of the coat were made with the quilt-as-you-go construction technique. The coat is an Yvonne Porcella haori pattern. See also Plate 70.*

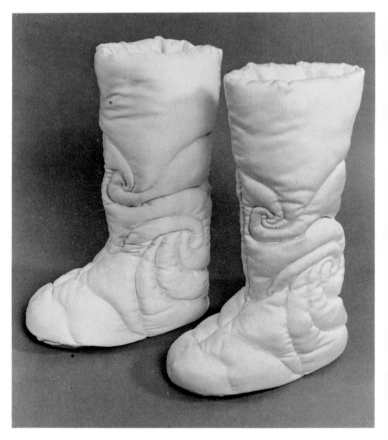

31. *"Cloud-hoppers," by Elsa Brown. These boots are made of off-white polyester fabric, trapunto stuffed with polyfil stuffing.*

Marjorie Murphy, on the other hand, does exquisite and elegant corded designs, which she combines with traditional quilting methods; a close look at her suit (*Photos 33a–c*) will show you what a professional she truly is.

In the 1970s quilts became known as "textile sandwiches." This expression, although descriptive, is vastly overworked and, aside from that, not altogether true. The phrase referred to the top and backing as the "bread" of the sandwich and the batting as the filler. A quilt does not always have to have a filler to be a quilt; a garment does not always have to have a filler to be a quilted garment.

Hundreds of years ago in Europe, and in Britain particularly, quilting with two layers was called "false quilting." Bulk and perhaps some warmth were eliminated, but the design was there. Many of Queen Elizabeth I's court robes were made this way, as were the gowns and robes from the Continent and the Far East. Japanese Sashiko quilting has no filler or middle layer. This is nothing new. I grew up with quilts, but we had two kinds, winter and summer quilts. The winter ones were "regular," but often the summer quilts had no filler. The top was simply quilted to the backing or lining, and it served as both a light cover and a spread. I've seen many similar examples in museums also.

Shadow quilting has been accepted without question,

32. *"Moth Jacket," by Elsa Brown. This jacket is hand-stamped, hand-quilted polyester crepe with polyfil stuffing.*

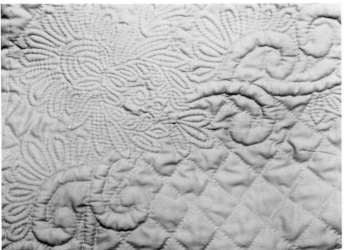

33c. *Detail of both trapunto and traditional quilting in Marjorie Murphy's suit.*

33a. (Above left) *Quilted suit, designed and made by Marjorie Murphy. The fabric is eggshell polyester–cotton broadcloth; the jacket and skirt are lined with peach. The entire suit is quilted by hand with exceptional workmanship, and the design emphasis is on trapunto.*

33b. (Above right) *Back view of Marjorie Murphy's suit jacket shows the trapunto work around the neck and hem and a fine traditional grid quilted in the body of the jacket.*

yet it has no filler, unless you consider the inserted designs as such. Shadow quilting consists of two layers of transparent fabric put together; this may be thin silk, voile, organdy, batiste, nylon, orlon, or something similar. Between the two layers you insert a design—traditionally a design cut from felt, but I see no reason why you couldn't use anything you wanted to. The quilting is a contoured stitching line that follows the design and also holds it in place. Shadow quilting could be used as elegant draperies or a room divider, but it could also become a breathtaking summer evening wrap fit for the most luxurious event.

We sacrifice some textural interest when we quilt without a filler, because it is loft that creates a lot of light and shadow interest. What we lose there, however, we can more than make up for in ease and intricacy of design and, perhaps, warm weather comfort. Thus, a filler is not always essential.

8

FILLERS AND BATTINGS

Nowadays, when we make quilts, we almost always use polyester batting, either needlepunched or traditional batts, with a glazed finish. Several companies produce these batts, and some quilt supply shops manufacture their own and sell them under brand names. Batts come in different thicknesses, but "regular" to thin batt is the usual choice in quiltmaking. This is also true of quilted garments, but here you have a greater choice of fillers and batts than you do in quilts, and you may also choose to use no filler at all. Your choice of fabrics is greater, too, and often the garment fabric you choose will help you to decide what filler to use. Fabric used for the shell can also be used as a filler. An evening jacket or coat, for instance, can be composed of several layers of chiffon, all of them different shades. The in-between layers act as filler, and you can quilt through all layers for a wonderful, ethereal effect.

Old-fashioned cotton battings are still available today, but they must be quilted very closely. They tear easily, and their position has almost been usurped by the newer polyester batts. However, they are responsible for some of the awe-inspiring antique quilts we admire so much—covered with exquisite feather wreaths and sprays, cables, and tiny diamond grids. Cotton batts are coming into favor for use in garments.

Polyester batts have much to recommend them. They are even and easy to quilt, they need not be quilted as closely as the cotton, and they can be either washed or dry cleaned. They also have one discouraging drawback: they beard, or pill. Little tiny strands of polyester work through the fabric. The official name for this is "fiber migration," and it has become an enormous problem to some of us and certainly to me. I like to work with solid colors, particularly with dark ones, and the bearding shows most on dark fabrics. In the past I have knocked myself out to make a "great garment," only to find out that it needed a shave when I was finished. If you pull on the little wisps sticking out, they keep coming out. The only solution is to clip them close to the fabric. This may be a solution, but it certainly is not the perfect one.

Bearding is not as pronounced on printed fabrics as it is on dyed ones—which are the solids—and it also shows far less on light colors than it does on dark. This happens to all-cotton fabrics as well as blends.

Tim Shackleford of Stearns and Foster Co. which makes Mountain Mist batts, says that each little polyester fiber is like a spring, forever pushing against the shell and trying to get free. Getting a batt with a glazed or bonded finish is some protection, since unbonded batts are far more likely to beard. Even after I understood what was causing the bearding, though, there wasn't a solution to it for a long time, and I finally resorted to adding a layer of batiste between shell and batting. The batiste is so thin it does not add any bulk in quilting, and it is so firmly woven that it makes the batt fibers behave. Now, though, there is a solution to bearding and we'll get to that in a page or two. Back to the choice of filler.

MUSLIN

Preshrunk, unbleached muslin is a good filler for lightweight garments. It has little or no loft but does add texture and body and is easy to quilt, either by hand or machine.

FLANNEL

Preshrunk cotton flannel is a firm, easy-to-quilt filler and adds some warmth, as well as a little weight. All-cotton flannel is difficult to find in stores today, for most of it has long since been blended with polyester and flame-retarding materials. I have solved that problem by buying all-cotton sheet-blankets, available at Sears, L. L. Bean (mail-order) in Maine, or the Country Store in Weston, Vermont. There is shrinkage involved, so be sure you wash them thoroughly before using. The Country Store also sells cotton flannel by the yard.

COTTON BATTING

As a natural fiber, cotton batting is comfortable to wear because it adjusts easily to body heat as well as to outside climate. It is easy to quilt, but, again, it must be closely quilted. I have used it for both hand and machine work and like the results very much. You must be careful when you unroll the batt since it tears so easily. Work on a flat surface, handle the batt gently, and pat it into place—then baste. This batt will not beard.

POLYESTER BATTING

Polyester batts (terylene in the U.K.) in many ways have revolutionized the popularity of quilting since the 1970s.

They have warmth and strength, they are even, and the most inexperienced quilter will find them easy to handle. They do not need to be quilted closely, can be quilted either by hand or machine, and are available either bonded or unbonded.

One of the newer types of polyester batt is the needle-punched batt, which is manufactured by a slightly different process than the others. Donna Wilder, of Fairfield Processing Co., maker of batts and fillers, describes it this way:

> [The] process consists of passing the blanket of fibers through a needling machine called a fiber locker. The machine has a multitude of barbed needles or hooks mounted on a grid which vibrates up and down. The blanket passes through, the needles pierce the blanket and entangle the fibers as they withdraw; thus, the fibers form the needlepunched batting.

The loft of polyester batts varies. The needlepunched batt I use is low and soft. Bonded battings, on the other hand, come as thick and high as you want. Both Fairfield's Ultraloft batt and Mountain Mist's Fat Batt are high loft; you can use them successfully not only in tied comforters but in tied garments, too. Yes, you can tie a garment in the same way you tie a quilt, if the filler is too thick for traditional or conventional quilting.

The Ok-lee Company makes a very good thin batting, which I also use (Ok-lee Quilting Co., P.O. Box 277, Oklee, Minnesota 56742).

COTTON CLASSIC

This is a newcomer to the field, developed by Fairfield Processing in answer to complaints about bearding. It also was developed specifically for use in quilted garments and has acquitted itself admirably in this area. Introduced early in 1980, its first major use was for the garments made by fabric artists and designers for the Houston Quilt Market show. I made two garments for that show and since then have used it frequently with increasing pleasure. It is a thin batting, 80 percent cotton and 20 percent polyester. It is even and does not have a great deal of loft, but in many garments this itself is a plus. It has a glaze on both sides and doesn't need a lot of basting to hold it in place. It quilts easily by machine, no bunching or balking, and I have enjoyed quilting it by hand. Only once did I think there was a little drag on the needle, but I was quilting in hot, humid weather, when I should have been at the beach or in the pool, and I think the humidity accounted for this. Needless to say, this batt does not beard, and that alone would endear it to me.

COTTON WADDINGS

In the United Kingdom you can buy a form of cotton domette interlining that is good for thin quilting, and there are
also other cotton waddings available. They are flatter, heavier, and more solid than synthetic types but they do not wash
as well.

POLYESTER FIBER

This is a loose fiber, manufactured by several companies and
marketed under different brand names. It is used primarily
for stuffing toys and pillows, but it also can be used for garments. Elsa Brown uses it in all her trapunto garments, and
it creates a lovely, puffy effect. Remember you use two layers of fabric for trapunto work, and a line of stitching
through both these layers makes a series of pockets. These
pockets are filled through a slit in the backing fabric, and
when all the stuffing is complete, the garment is lined.

POLYESTER FLEECE

This is a fairly firm felted material and has been used frequently in making the strip- or string-quilted vests popular
in the past few years. It seems to work in vests, but it is stiff
and does not conform to the body the way I think a garment
should, and I prefer to save it for tote bags and placemats.

OTHER SYNTHETICS (U.K.)

Besides the bouncy terylene wadding mentioned above, you
can buy Courtelle (acrylic) wadding, which is quite thin but
can be used in several layers. A thicker, denser synthetic
wadding is Tricel or cellulose triacetate. It is papery on one
side and fluffy on the other, and you should place the papery side against the back of your fabric when quilting. Bor-
dalex is another firm, dense synthetic wadding used for
upholstery but ideal for machine quilting.

WOOL BATTS

We don't hear a lot about wool batts, perhaps because they
are not readily available and also because they are expensive, but in some ways they are the ultimate batt to use in a
quilted garment, for here you have warmth without weight.
These batts, like the cotton ones, are natural fibers that are

soft, drapable, and very easy to quilt. They come with or without a fabric or cheesecloth cover, but I suggest you get the covered one. The batts are already moth-proofed, and come in different sizes and weights. Jean Dubois in her book *The Wool Quilt* says batts can be ordered from Rastetter Woolen Mill, Route 62, Millersburg, Ohio 44654. Donna Wilder adds another source, Frankenmuth Woolen Mills, 570 South Main Street, Frankenmuth, Michigan 48734, and Carter Houck adds Bemidji Woolen Mills, Bemidji, Minnesota 56601.

In the United Kingdom the traditional wool wadding is sheep's fleece. Another is domette, which has an open, fluffy structure and is warm without being too bulky, which makes it ideal for quilted clothes.

SILK WADDING

Silk wadding from Japan is increasingly available. It must be shaped by hand, but it is excellent for use in garments.

AN OLD SOFT BLANKET

You had no idea there were so many fillers, did you? But a blanket can be given new life if used as a filler in a quilted garment. You may have such a blanket around the house, somewhat worn, faded, and either relegated for camping or hidden under the new quilt on the bed because its appearance isn't what it once was. Wool blankets are especially admirable for use in garments, but a worn cotton one might do as well.

All of the fillers I've mentioned may be used with either hand or machine stitching with equal success; the choice is yours.

9
QUILTING: HAND AND MACHINE

Before you begin making your quilted garment, you still have a few choices, or rather decisions, ahead of you.

By this time you should know if your garment is to be reversible. If so, you'll be quilting through the lining as you quilt the shell. You can quilt this way, with the garment lining as backing, even if your garment is not reversible. You can quilt through shell and filler only, then line the garment when the quilting is done and the body seams joined.

You also need to have a quilting design in mind, and you should know how you're going to mark it on the fabric. And you should give a thought—or two thoughts—to how you will finish the seams and the outside edges. Sometimes you can't, or shouldn't, wait until the last minute to work these things out.

It's just as important to have a good quilting design as it is to have a good pieced or appliquéd design; quilting can be subordinate to other design, or it can be the star of the show. Some pieced designs may need only outline quilting around each shape, and this is also true of appliqué. Some pieced designs, especially if composed of straight-line piecing, look wonderful when quilted with curves; this pattern on top of pattern adds extra depth.

One of the easiest quilting designs, no matter how the shell is decorated, is channel quilting, which is simply vertical lines, evenly spaced. Many prequilted fabrics on sale in shops are channel quilted; others are zigzag quilted or quilted in a diamond grid. I like to quilt my clothes with designs, even simple lines, that won't be mistaken for commercial work. I have nothing against these prequilted fabrics; many of them are stunning, well-quilted, and of good quality fabric, but if you are making your own garment "from scratch," it is a shame to deny yourself the pleasure of doing your own quilting. I've used the prequilted fabric several times—once for a robe, once for a gift jacket when I was in a hurry, and a couple of times as linings for coats.

At any rate, you can do your own channel quilting either by hand or machine. For a different look, try double-needle stitching on the machine, using two different color threads.

Another effective but uncomplicated design is an all-over grid, either square or diamond shaped. You can also quilt in circles, interlocking or concentric, or use the clam-

Fig. 31. *Ten ideas for quilting a garment, either by hand or machine. Two or more patterns could be combined in one garment.*

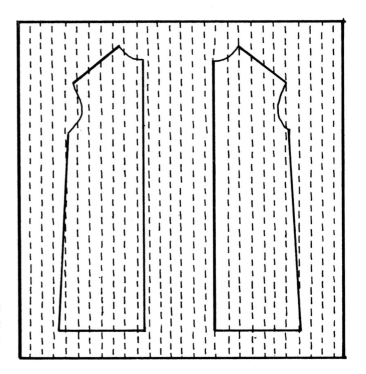

Fig. 32. *Channel-quilted fabric yardage with pattern pieces in place for cutting. This may be commercially quilted fabric, or machine quilted by you.*

34. *Red quilted coat, by Barbara O'Connor. The coat is all hand quilted, with borders of hearts around the sleeves and hem.*

shell or teacup quilting design as an all-over quilting pattern for your garment. All of these, used with pieced work or appliqué designs, are effective. Contour or echo quilting often is used effectively for appliqué designs, with the lines sometimes filling the whole area and other times confined to the appliqué shapes themselves or perhaps an inch or so outside. Quilting designs can be mixed and matched as easily as pieced or appliqué designs can.

Emphasis in this book so far has been placed on creating a special design for the shell of your garment using pattern and color, but I want to remind you that an all-quilted or "whole-cloth" garment is an elegant and classic statement, always in good taste, always in good fashion. Many connoisseurs regard antique white-work quilts as the ultimate examples, since the design depends on the skill and expertise of the quilter alone. Such quilts—and such garments—raise quilting to its highest level.

In planning a design for an all-quilted garment, take advantage of contrasts, not only in line but in pattern as well.

You can quilt intricate motifs or patterns, then fill in; you can quilt feathers and cables up and down or around your coat or jacket; you can quilt with random or meander quilting, so close that the fabric looks stippled when you've finished. The lining of such a coat could be the same color but in a different texture. It also could be pieced, or you could simply sew two or three lengths of patterned or plain fabric together to create yardage for the lining.

Some quilted designs should be marked on the fabric shell or lining before the garment is assembled with filler; at other times, you can mark as you go. For instance, my "Midnight Garden" black cotton cape (*Plate 71*) is lined with Concord's large floral print "Sumatra." I quilted the cape from the lining side, using the floral motifs as a quilting design. My batiked coat "Purple Passion" (*Plates 66 and 67*) is contour quilted by hand following the batik pattern. I lined the coat with a rusty red cotton brocade, and the quilting design shows up beautifully on this solid color. "Morning Mist" (*Plate 70*), the reversible gray cotton haori coat, is solid gray on one side and pieced on the other (see also photo on page 90). I quilted from the solid gray side, using one of Helen Squire's scrolled patterns, and it is very effective superimposed on the piecing.

MARKING A QUILTING DESIGN

Transferring a quilting design to fabric is often difficult. I've seen many an otherwise lovely quilt or garment ruined with smudged pencil lines that can't be removed. Soft lead pencils are the worst offenders, and it is a good idea to stay away from them.

If your quilting design is a straight-line one, use masking tape. Lay the tape along the quilting lines, and stitch on both sides of it; the space between the lines is determined by the width of the tape. When each line is quilted, peel off the tape gently. If you are working with a napped fabric, pull *with* the nap and not against it.

If I am machine quilting, I put the tape a quarter of an inch to the left of the quilting line so that the presser foot does not ride down the fabric on top of the tape. Instead, the left edge of the foot is just against the edge of the tape, and in this way the tape isn't pressed into the fabric.

If you have stencils or templates for your quilting design, use a white charcoal pencil or silver Col-erase pencil (Caran d'ache in the U.K.) for dark fabrics and a no. 3 (or 2H) hard lead pencil for light ones. Also, try transfering the design with dotted lines instead of a continuous line. You can also try a chalk pencil or a soap sliver. If you are working with very delicate fabric or one difficult to mark, thread

35b. *Detail of quilting on the back of Barbara O'Connor's vest.*

35a. *Back view of white quilted vest, by Barbara O'Connor. A single large heart and intertwined hearts are hand quilted as the focal point. The background is quilted in a diagonal grid.*

baste around your template. I used this method with the jacket of "Night in India" (*Plate 68*), the evening outfit I made from an Indian silk sari. Thread baste around the outside design line, then follow subsequent lines by eye.

You can also transfer a design using the light method, but this must be done before your garment is assembled for quilting. Draw the design with heavy marking pen on paper, and position your fabric over this, being careful about the placement. Pin paper and fabric together. You can use the stand-up method and natural light and work in daytime with a door or window; or you can use the sit-down method and transfer your design with a light box, either purchased or homemade.

I do not use dressmaker's carbon or a tracing wheel; I did try them out, but it seems difficult to me to get an accurate tracing. Also, the tracing wheels, whether round or serrated, are too sharp to use safely; if you apply any pressure at all you may cut or damage your fabric.

Nor do I use the water-soluble pens to mark a quilting design. I have used them occasionally and with good results, and many of my friends use them all the time, but to me they are a consumer-beware item. You need to get your fabric quite wet in order to remove the marks, and I'm not always willing to do that. Also, if you're impatient and press the work before it is completely dry, the heat from the iron will set the marks permanently, as will the use of detergent. All in all, to me the hazards outweigh the advantages.

An easy and popular way to mark for machine quilting is to draw your design on paper, position the paper on either the shell or lining, and then machine stitch through the paper. It's sometimes a little messy to remove all the bits of paper from the stitching later on, but it is an easy and accurate way to work, and you need not worry at all about marking on the fabric. I first stumbled on stitching or quilting

36. *Quilted yoke on jacket, by Katie Pasquini. The jacket is white silk, and the yoke is purple raw silk, designed butterfly fashion to extend toward the shoulders and down the front and hand quilted to bring out detail. Jacket is shown over a blouse that goes with it. Purple silk pants complete the outfit.*

through paper many years ago, when a friend of mine brought back a coat she had purchased in Hong Kong. The coat collar and band down the front were heavily quilted in curlicues; we snipped the lining free at the hem edge of the coat for a good look inside and found the paper still there!

You may not need or want a specific quilting design at all. Instead you can baste your layers together and let the stitches fall where they may, meandering at will over the fabric surface.

An unusual type of quilting design—especially for an all-quilted garment—is a drawing or illustration. It could be people, a landscape or cityscape, a garden, or a jungle scene. Marilyn Price used this most effectively with her "People Quilt" (*Photo 42*). The design, stitched with dark thread, stands out dramatically, but it also serves as the quilting design that holds the coat layers together.

WORKING IN SECTIONS

Whether you quilt by hand or machine, it is easier to do it in sections, for then the work is flat; the sections can be joined together later in any of several different ways. Before you begin, however, think of how the outside edges will be finished. If bound, or finished with a band, that's done when

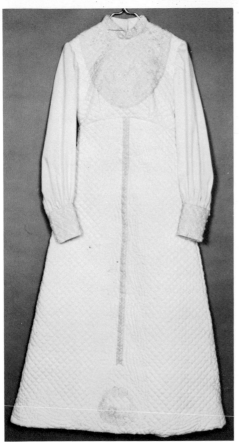

37. *"Arsenic and Old Lace," a hand-quilted dress of eggshell poly-cotton, by Mildred Guthrie. Dress has a yoke of antique lace, and Mildred covered peas with silk to use as buttons. She says Dolley Madison used covered peas as buttons on one of her garments. The bodice is quilted without filler.*

the quilting is finished. If, however, you want a seamed edge on a reversible garment, you'll have to take care of this before you do the quilting. For instance, if you want a seamed edge around the neck and front openings of a vest, jacket, or coat, stitch these seams first. You can still do this piecemeal, or in sections. Take the front shell section and put it on top of the filler or batt, cut to size. Now put the lining on top of the shell, right sides together. Pin all this in place, and stitch from the shoulder down the front and around the bottom edge to the side bottom, allowing a half-inch (12 mm) seam. Trim the batting back close to the stitching line, then turn this section so it is properly assembled with shell, batt, and lining. Beginning at the seamed outside edges, smooth the layers, then baste securely and go ahead with your quilting. When each section has been seamed and quilted, only the shoulder and side seams need to be joined and the sleeves added. This is what we call lining to the edge.

Otherwise, baste each section together with shell, batt, and lining. I think thread basting is safer than pin basting, and the basting will stay in place until you want to get rid of it. Sometimes the pins don't. When you quilt through these three layers, of course, the quilting design will show on the lining side, whether or not the garment is reversible.

If you want to line the garment separately, you need only do the quilting through shell and batt or filler; a backing is unnecessary.

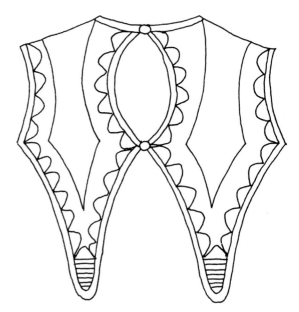

Fig. 34. *Quilted collar to wear on a dress or an outer garment.*

Fig. 33. *Rows of quilting accent the sleeve and hem borders on a coat.*

HAND QUILTING
THE GARMENT SECTION

Choose the thread first, then the needle to fit. You can use regular quilting thread, heavy duty thread, regular sewing thread either single or double, perle cotton, embroidery floss, or metallic thread. Chances are you won't be using a quilt frame but you can use a quilting hoop if you are more comfortable working this way. I use a fourteen-inch (36-cm) hoop because it's large enough to keep me busy for a while and is a convenient size for travel (fitting comfortably in a suitcase or a tote bag). I also do a lot of lap quilting, and often I work on a table, without a hoop of any kind.

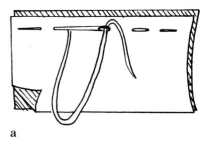

a

When you quilt a garment, you have a wider choice of thread than you would if you were working on a quilt. You also have a wider choice of stitches and spacing. I saw some early Chinese silk robes from the collection of the Metropolitan Museum of Art in New York, and many of these were quilted with silk floss, with stitches almost an inch (2.5 cm) apart. The needle slipped through the batting or wadding from stitch to stitch, and the final effect was like a dotted grid. In other robes, the stitches were long, a half-inch (12 mm) or so in length.

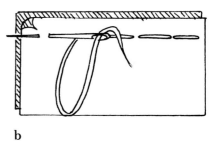

b

You start and stop your quilting in a garment the same way you do for a quilt, so that each end of the thread is buried forever (you hope) in the middle and no one can see where you began or ended. If you are quilting through batting only and plan to line the garment later, you need not worry about this since the back will never show. Use knots if you want to; I'll never tell. If you are hand quilting through the lining and want to finish the body seams with a quilt-as-you-go technique, then stop quilting about an inch (2.5 cm) from the edge.

Depending on fabric and design, you might like to try quilting with an embroidery stitch—feather or herringbone, for instance, or a combination of several. Since a quilting stitch is defined as one that holds the layers together, you can include tying too; a tied stitch performs its duty as well as a running stitch. You can tie with a square knot, with buttons, tassels, bows, beads, or sequins. Try it on a test piece first and see which appeals to you.

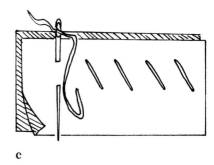

c

Fig. 35. *Preparing shell, filler, and lining layers for quilting: (a) even basting stitches; (b) uneven basting stitches; (c) diagonal basting stitches.*

MACHINE QUILTING

For many of you quilters, the sewing machine may be a foreign object, and a maligned one at that. For years there has been such preference for and such snobbery about hand quilting that you might not want to come right out and defend machine work unless you don't mind being tarred and

38a. *Back view of a quilted vest, by Alison Goss. The fabric is hand-quilted Chinese silk brocade.*

38b. *Detail of quilting on Alison Goss's vest.*

feathered. Hand quilting may still be queen of the May, but that doesn't mean we can't accord machine quilting its rightful place. It isn't a substitute for hand quilting at all; it is an entirely different technique, and the results are also entirely different. Some very fine antique quilts have been machine quilted—and beautifully. One lady in the late 1800s was so proud of her new machine—and wanted everyone to know she had one—that she not only used it to quilt her quilt but used a contrasting thread so everyone would be sure to notice the stitching!

Many exquisite garments have also been machine quilted; the examples I've seen call for respect and admiration and not disdain or contempt. Well-known couturiers, from both Europe and America, have used machine quilting for exquisite designs in luxurious garments, and many of today's couture offerings are machine quilted.

Machine quilting a garment is a lot easier than machine quilting a quilt. The bulk alone of a quilt would be a deterrent, and happily that isn't a problem with garments. As in hand quilting, however, I still prefer to machine quilt in sections, then join the sections later whenever possible.

Basting, important as it is, is even more important for machine quilting. The last thing you want to happen is to have the layers of fabric moving in opposite directions as you are stitching. A mistake is more difficult to correct with machine quilting than with hand quilting because the stitches are more difficult to remove and they often leave needle holes in the fabric. Along with basting, it's important to try a sample or two before you tackle the real thing, especially if you are using anything other than regular sewing thread.

As you know, thread is important. You can quilt on the machine with quilting thread, regular thread, or silk thread. You can also use metallic thread, buttonhole twist, or a very fine crochet cotton. If these go through the needle assembly, fine; if not, wind the bobbin with them, which means quilting from the lining side instead of the shell.

The right needle is important too. First, it should be new and sharp; and second, it should be the right size for the thread you're using. Buttonhole twist and metallic threads both have a tendency to fray, or untwist, and the needle must be the right size to accommodate it. Also, for these threads loosen the needle tension a little bit; it takes some of the fight out of the thread.

I guess I have quilted a couple of hundred miles on my machines, and I want to pass on to you every tip I can think of. Almost all of the quilting books and magazines emphasize hand quilting, and very little has been written on machine quilting, so I'm sure this will be a help to you and, perhaps, save you from making many of the mistakes I have.

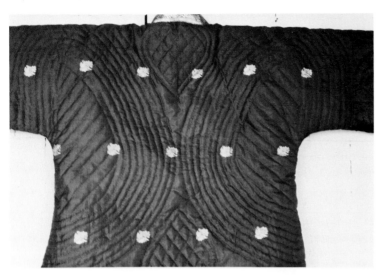

39. *Detail of back of a jacket, by the author, showing quilting. The fabric is silk from an Indian sari, hand quilted with silk thread.*

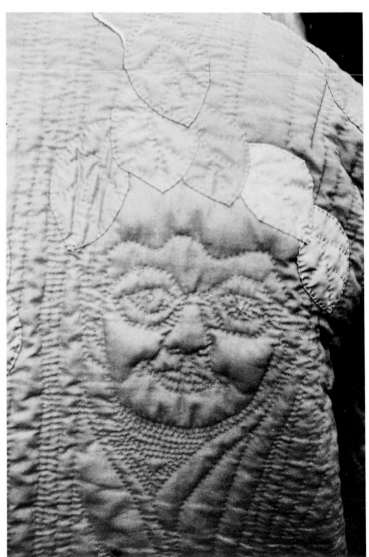

40. *Detail of back of a quilted jacket, by Marilyn Clark, showing her quilted self-portrait. She wears a crown of leaves in shades of rust, red, and green appliquéd to brown cotton. The jacket is entirely hand quilted.*

1. Remember to baste and try some sample stitching.
2. In addition to basting, use pins for some quilting lines, especially curved ones. Pin every quarter-inch or so at right angles at to the quilting line and pull the pins out as you come to them—don't sew over them.
3. Check the pressure of your machine. On an old model, this may be a screw on top of the machine head, on the left side. On a newer model, there is a little wheel inside the little door on the left of the machine. You want to loosen the pressure to give you a little more room under the presser foot. Remember that a sewing machine is geared to handle two layers of fabric of medium weight, which represents most home sewing. Newer machines will adjust pressure automatically, but don't take this for granted when quilting. A layer of batting between the shell and lining of your garment is often too much. The machine balks, and one or more layers will pile up and wrinkle. Test the pressure of your machine with samples of the actual fabrics and fillers you are using for your garment.
4. Check the tensions of your machine and be sure the stitch is balanced. Most of the time I am able to machine quilt without touching either tension, but when using metallic thread or buttonhole twist I find it helps to loosen the needle tension very slightly. I *never* touch the bobbin tension. I did once and finally ended up taking the machine to the repairman, where it stayed for a couple of weeks while he got it balanced for me. The bobbin tension is never-never land.
5. Be sure your machine is clean and free of lint and that the bobbin is full. It's exasperating to run out of bobbin thread halfway down a quilting line; you may not even know it until you come to the end, and then there are those loose threads in the middle where they shouldn't be. In my opinion, if and when this happens, it is easier to take out the quilting line and start over again.
6. Try the straight-stitch presser foot instead of the zigzag foot. The smaller needle hole sometimes prevents fabric from going down and getting caught.
7. Try a quilting foot, if you have one, or a button foot. Both of these have the toes cut off and let you see where you're going.
8. Keep a notebook and sample sheet handy. Test out quilting with different combinations of threads and needles and include with this samples of different stitch lengths. I prefer a longer stitch; I think it looks better, and the shorter stitches seem to sink into fabric. A stitch length of 8 to 10 on the Singer and 4 on the Viking are both good for the quilting I do.
9. I use the presser foot when I machine quilt rather than drop the feed for free-machine quilting. I feel I have

41. *"Red Band," designed and made by Marilyn Price of her own hand-dyed and hand-printed velvet. Marilyn used an eraser print on the sleeves and hem, which are piped in red. The coat is machine quilted with polyester batt. Photo by Marilyn Price.*

more control over what I'm doing. You might want to try both methods and see which is best for you.

10. When you quilt a sample, make it large enough for accurate testing. Put your machine in reduction gear, if you have one. If after following the above suggestions your quilt layers are bunching up on you or not behaving properly, try a stabilizer. This sounds important and it is. Slip paper underneath the bottom layer—tissue paper, tracing paper, typing paper or shelf paper. It may give you the smooth road bed you need for your travels. Tear it away when you're finished; most of it will come off easily since it is already perforated, but little bits of paper may cling to the stitching. If it is on the lining or shell side, you can remove it with tweezers. If these little bits are on batting or filler and will be covered up later, don't do anything about them; they won't do any damage.

11. Another aid to stabilizing—and one that may work without paper or anything else—is an even-feed attachment or a walking foot. They are practically the same but have different names for different machines.

Their purpose is to see that all layers feed through the presser foot, or under it, at the same speed.

12. I've already mentioned using masking tape to mark straight lines for quilting, but be sure to place these on the fabric so that the presser foot rides alongside one edge of the tape and not on top of it. Measure the distance from the needle to the outside edge of the presser foot, and put the tape along this line.

13. If a quilting guide came with your machine, try it for straight-line quilting. It may be all the marking you need.

14. Pull three or four inches (7–10 cm) of thread, both needle and bobbin, to the back when you start to quilt, and hang on to the threads until you've taken the first two or three stitches; this gets you off to a nice clean start. Leave a few inches when you stop, too, if you've stopped *inside* the garment section and not on the edge. If you are quilting through the lining, you don't want anyone to see where you stopped. Thread a hand-sewing needle with the needle thread, run it through the filler, bring it out an inch or more away, and clip it. Do the same with the bobbin thread; the little tails will sink back inside and no one will ever know. If you feel the need of a little more security, tie a tiny knot in the thread close to the fabric; the knot will pull through along with the rest of the thread and lie snug and safe in the batting.

Study your quilt design—or designs—before you start to quilt. It's like looking at a road map; you want to stitch as far as possible without stopping. If your design is not continuous, you may not be able to take advantage of this step, but it is worth considering. When you turn a corner in quilting, leave the needle in the fabric layers, lift the presser foot, pivot the fabric, then lower the presser foot and quilt the next line.

You can quilt circles with the presser foot on if you go slowly and the circles aren't too small. If you are itching to try free-machine quilting, this is the place. Read the instruction book, and use a hoop if it is suggested. However, I find the hoop a hindrance in machine quilting since you are limited too sharply by the edges of the hoop. Try quilting without the hoop, and learn to maneuver your fabric layers smoothly. Keep both hands flat on the work, guiding it. There's no substitute for practice. When you drop the feed dog, don't get rid of all the pressure because some of it will help hold the fabric. This technique may be in your instruction book under "darning," so read that section too.

If you've basted as well as you should have, it won't make any difference whether you start quilting from the

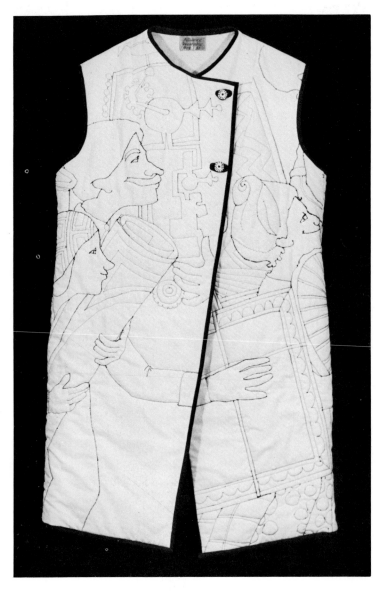

42. *"People Quilt," designed and made by Marilyn Price. The design was drawn directly on the poly–cotton blend fabric, then machine quilted through shell, batt, and lining using a small zigzag stitch. The buttons are hand-made ceramic. Photo by Marilyn Price.*

center out or from one side across the width of the garment section. Where possible, it's a good idea to do your stitching in the same direction; otherwise there may be some wrinkles on the other side. When you finish a line of quilting, turn the work over and take a good look at it; be sure there has been no shifting or puckering. Sometimes, no matter how careful you are, some stitching will have to come out. Use your seam ripper—carefully; slide it under every third or fourth stitch on one side and cut the thread. Now pull the long uncut thread; it should come free. You still have all those little stitches poking up from the fabric, but a little masking tape laid on top of them will do the trick. Just lift up the tape, and the threads will come with it.

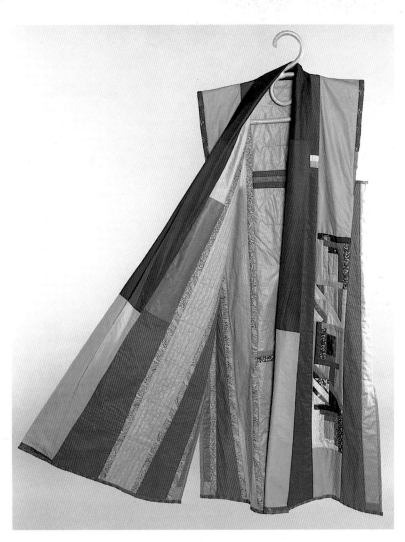

Plate 48. *Tibetan coat, by Beth Gutcheon, Porcella pattern. Cottons and polished cottons, reversible; polyester batt, outline quilted.*

Plate 49. *Back view of Tibetan coat.*

Plate 50. *Blue cotton quilted coat, by Marjorie Puckett. Appliqués were cut from strip-pieced fabric and piped in red; machine quilting was done in red thread. Adaptation of Folkwear Turkish coat pattern.*

Plate 51. *Back view of Ostrich Coat, by Marjorie Puckett. White cotton is appliquéd with various fabrics, machine quilted, and lined in red.*

Plate 52. *Princess Vest, by Dorothy Lazara. Two royal figures take up entire side fronts of vest, and on the back a sinister queen holds court in a hallway.*

Plate 53. *Chinese Jacket, by Dorothy La-*
zara. The figures on the front are of a god
and goddess popular in Chinese religion.

Plate 54. *Back view of Chinese Jacket.*
Shown is a Buddha on his throne; on each
side are warriors, copies of life-size sculp-
tures that were buried with emperors.
Shoulders have Bugaku masks, used in
Chinese operas, as appliqués. The color
red symbolizes a good, holy person, and
black symbolizes a long life.

Plate 55. *Quilted cotton jacket, by Judy Math-*
ieson. An antique mola is used on back as a fo-
cal point.

Plate 56. *Front view of quilted cotton jacket,*
by Judy Mathieson, embellished with coins,
shi-sha mirrors, and beads.

Plate 57. *Zigzag jacket, by Marilyn Price, back view. Body is batiked cotton, machine quilted. The medallion on the back is embroidered and couched. Sleeves are pieced of solid-color cotton strips. Jacket is lined with white satin, and buttons are covered in the same fabric as the binding.*

Plate 58. *Appliquéd quilted coat, by Jo Diggs. Shown is detail of front top section.*

Plate 59. *Sleeve detail of Jo Diggs's appliquéd quilted coat.*

Plate 60. Left: *Black Magic Dream Vest, by Liz Surbeck, appliquéd and quilted. Batiks, various other fabrics, and antique lace are used with a variety of baubles for embellishment. Vest also has trapunto quilting.*

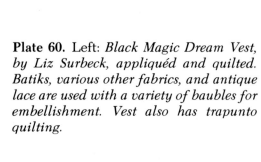

Plate 61. Right: *Back view of Black Magic Dream Vest.*

Plate 62. *Long quilted cotton lounge robe, by Harriet A. Thornton. There is a hidden zipper in front, and the back design is identical.*

Plate 63. *Pieced and quilted cotton jacket, by Harriet A. Thornton, back view. Sleeves can be folded back to make deep cuffs.*

Plate 64. *Lightning Strikes Twice, author, a black cotton coat, machine quilted with both single and double needles. Front band is pieced with various fabrics. Sleeves are red cotton; right sleeve is decorated with yo-yos and baubles, and left with Seminole patchwork bands.*

Plate 65. *Back view of Lightning Strikes Twice.*

Plate 66. *Purple Passion, designed and made by the author. Design was drawn on unbleached muslin, batiked by Tipi Halsey, and hand quilted by the author. Lined with red cotton brocade. A Folkwear Turkish coat pattern.*

Plate 67. *Back view of Purple Passion.*

Plate 68. *Night in India, evening dress and quilted jacket, designed and made by the author from a silk Indian sari. Jacket is cut mandarin-style, hand quilted with silk thread, collared with gold woven band, and fastened with ties.*

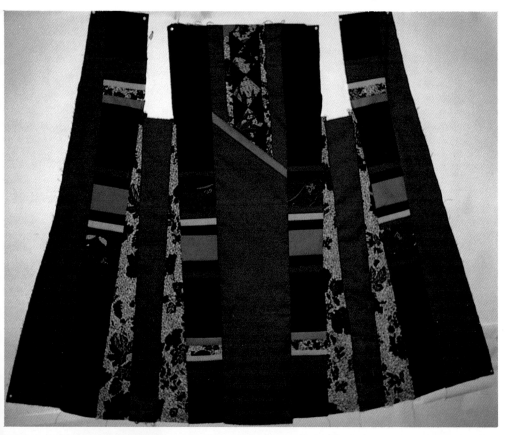

Plate 69. *Tibetan coat in progress, by the author. Shown is lining side, pieced with various cottons. Outer shell is pieced of cotton and velveteen (Crompton). Each side is machine quilted separately to batting, then joined and finished with front band.*

Plate 70. *Morning Mist, by the author. Reversible haori coat. Outside is pieced with random design; the inside is of solid gray cotton. Hand quilted with Cotton Classic from Fairfield Processing. Porcella pattern.*

Plate 71. *Midnight Garden, by the author. Black cotton cape, hand quilted, with printed floral motifs appliquéd to cape edge, couched with black yarn. Cape is lined with same floral print (Concord fabrics) and filled with Cotton Classic.*

Plate 72. *Evening outfit, by Katie Pasquini, of hand-dyed silk. Pants are purple raw silk, with same silk used as cape-collar and cuff trim, padded and hand-quilted. Jacket is white silk; the blouse is blue silk with quilted band closing.*

If you are contour quilting around a preprinted design, don't feel you have to stitch around every little curve or angle; simplify overly detailed designs; the effect will be just as good.

Your hands are important tools in machine quilting. Use both of them, flat against your fabric, to give it a little tension and to hold it in place as you stitch. I mentioned this with free-machine quilting, but it is just as important in presser-foot quilting. Also, if the garment sections are heavy enough to slide off the machine bed, use a chair or card table next to it to support the weight.

If the work needs pressing when you've finished quilting, use a little steam instead to remove any wrinkles. Get your iron hot with a good head of steam, and hold it over the quilted section without touching the fabric. This probably won't be necessary if you pressed the shell and lining before you put them together. There are special little puff irons on the market now, made specifically to steam out wrinkles. It is nice to have one in addition to a steam iron.

43. *Short-sleeved quilted silk garment, by Sas Colby, back view. Figures are drawn, then machine quilted through shell, batt, and lining. Hand stitching on the front of the garment accentuates the figures.*

You can quilt with double or twin needles for a wonderful effect, but don't do it if you are quilting through the lining where the quilting will be visible. These needles are mounted on one shank, set an eighth of an inch or less apart, and use one bobbin, so that the underside of the quilting has a zigzag instead of the double lines.

And, speaking of a zigzag, you can quilt with this stitch if you like. Do some samples of the stitch and try different widths and different lengths. If your machine has built-in decorative stitches, or if you have them mounted on cams, try these for effect. Try a satin stitch for certain designs; it produces a heavy solid line and makes a design stand out.

You should experiment with different threads and different fabrics in your machine quilting. I mentioned buttonhole twist and metallic thread in the needle assembly and suggested you loosen the tension very slightly. You should use a larger needle to discourage the thread fraying or untwisting. I have two machines, Singer Touch and Sew and a Viking 6020, and when I use either of these heavier threads I use a 16 or an 18 with the Singer and 90 or 100 for the Viking. If after this you have problems, then wind the bobbin with the heavier thread, use regular sewing thread in the needle, and do your quilting from the batting or backing side. When you make this switch, remember to put the needle tension back to normal—and don't touch the bobbin tension.

You can machine quilt delicate fabrics, silks and satins, and even chiffons and organzas. In Chapters 4 and 5 on pieced and appliquéd designs, I talked about Ultrasuede fabric and coated fabrics. These can be quilted beautifully, but they are easier to machine quilt than hand quilt because of the density of the fabric. Remember that Ultrasuede fabric is a napped fabric, and you should stitch with the nap and not against it. I do think an even-feed or walking-foot attachment helps when you quilt these special fabrics. Also, you may need to slip paper between the fabric layers and the bed of the machine. You will have to test these out on your own machine before you can decide what action to take.

It is too difficult to finish body seams (side, shoulder, whatever) with a quilt-as-you-go technique if you machine quilt, for you would need to stop quilting an inch from the cut edge. When machine quilting, you're better off to start your stitching at the outside edge, go to the other edge, and finish your seams with binding.

When you are machine quilting from edge to edge, you don't need to worry about the thread ends. They don't need to be tied off because they will eventually be secured in a seam. If while quilting your design you must start or stop somewhere inside the garment section you're working on, then you must secure the thread ends. If you are quilting through shell and batt only, turn the work over, tug on the bobbin thread until you see the loop the needle thread makes, then pull it through and tie both of them together to secure.

You can't tie thread ends this way if you are quilting through the lining, however, because they would show. Slip the work from under the presser foot, and thread a hand-sewing or quilting needle with each thread in turn: two needle threads on top, two bobbin threads underneath. Finish these off as you would for hand quilting, and run the thread ends into the filler.

Half the fun in machine quilting is experimenting. I mentioned channel quilting earlier in this chapter, and for one of the jackets I made, I channel quilted the lining to Cotton Classic batt by machine. The vertical lines were about an inch and a quarter (3 cm) apart. When this was finished, I put the shell over the quilted lining and machine quilted again from the shell side. The shell was pieced, and I followed the shapes of the piecing—but the pattern that showed up on the lining side was a fascinating maze of lines. You could do the same thing in strip quilting: prequilt your lining to the batt, then use this as a foundation as you strip quilt, perhaps diagonally.

44. *Evening jacket, by Marjorie Puckett. This stunning, fitted, waist-length jacket is made of a prequilted black knit fabric and decorated with a varicolored ribbon ruching around wrists and neck and down the front. Ribbons are satin, velvet, grosgrain, and brocade, all of different widths. The commercially quilted fabric has a zigzag design.*

10

THE BIG WRAPUP: GETTING IT ALL TOGETHER

Department stores for years have used the phrase "ready to wear," or, more recently, *prêt à porter*. It means, of course, that the clothes they have for sale are ready for you to put on and wear. I think "ready to wear" fits neatly into our lives when we are working on quilted clothes. You're in the final phase, now, sewing up construction seams and finishing the edges, and before you know it your masterpiece will truly be ready to wear. The final steps are usually a combination of machine and hand stitching, and these often depend on the garment and the final effect you want.

When the quilting is finished, and before you join the sections together, it is a good idea to check each section as to cut and size. Get out the paper or muslin pattern, and lay the pattern on top of the fabric. You may need to trim a little here and there. Also, if you have simply quilted yardage for your garment, this is the time to do the major cutting. Accuracy in cutting is important because it helps in accurate seaming. Don't cut notches in your seams for matching unless you plan to cover the seams with binding. Notches do help in matching a seam, but cut them outward, or, better yet, mark the place with a safety pin or a tailor tack.

QUILT-AS-YOU-GO METHOD OF FINISHING SEAMS

You can only finish seams with the quilt-as-you-go method if you have hand quilted each garment section and stopped the quilting about an inch from the outside edges. Put two of the sections together, right sides inside. For instance, two fronts would be placed against the back section, with right sides facing each other. You now work with only the shell layers of fabric; pin the batting and lining out of the way. Match the seam edges of the shells, then machine stitch, using a half-inch seam allowance. These seams include shoulder and side seams and any other unstitched seams within the body of the garment. When stitching is done, turn garment shell side down on your work table, and finger press the seams open. At this point you will probably have to trim the batting a little bit so it won't overlap; the edges should abut. If you won't be quilting over these seams later, sew or lace the batting edges together lightly. Now smooth one edge of the lining over the batting, turn under the seam allowance of the other lining section, and pin it in place over lining and batt. Usually, the front lining section will go over the back lining so that the final hand seam is toward the back. This is true of both shoulder and side seams.

When the lining is pinned in place, slip stitch it by hand. Each body seam should be completely sewed before the edges are bound.

For a vest, you need only to finish the outside and armhole edges with binding. If you are working on a jacket or coat, you must finish the sleeves and attach them using the same quilt-as-you-go finish. Fold the sleeve in half with the right side inside, then stitch through only the shell layers. Trim the batt if necessary, and finish the sleeve seam by hand. Pin the sleeves into the armhole, easing it to fit, then machine stitch with the sleeve on top. Do not fingerpress this seam open, however. Trim batting back closely, then hand sew the sleeve lining over these raw edges, using the machine stitched line as a guide. This trimmed seam allowance will be pointed toward the sleeve cap.

The quilt-as-you-go method should only be used with hand-quilted sections because it is time consuming to try it with machine quilting if your quilting has a definite design. Since you must stop an inch (2.5 cm) short of the outside, you would have to "get rid of" all the thread ends before you could finish the seams. Also, if you needed to continue quilting over the seam it would be more difficult in machine work to be exact in picking up the stitching line where you left off, and you would have added work getting rid of thread ends. Even if you need additional stitching to cover seams in hand quilting, it is far easier to cope with. The exception to this is a machine-quilted section where the quilting is contained within the body of the garment piece and doesn't come that close to the edges.

Instead of hand finishing the seam with a slip stitch, you can fold under the seam allowance of the lining and topstitch it in place by machine. This is in keeping with the quilting technique you have used.

The hand-finished quilt-as-you-go method is a neat and easy way to handle your construction seams. It works just as well for a reversible garment as for one that is not.

FLAT-FELLED SEAMS

Flat felling is similar to the quilt-as-you-go method except that, instead of stitching only the shell layers together, you stitch through *all* layers—six of them. You can fell the seam on either the outside or the lining side. When the seam is

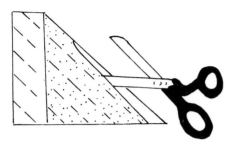

Fig. 36a. *Cutting bias strips for tape or tubing.*

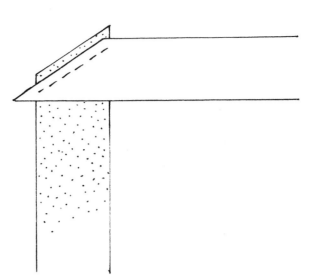

Fig. 36b. *Joining two bias strips on straight grain of fabric.*

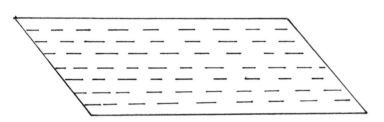

Fig. 36c. *Marking fabric for continuous bias.*

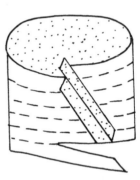

Fig. 36d. *Seaming and cutting for continuous bias. Notice offset by one width.*

stitched, you need to trim the fabric and batting closely except for the one seam allowance to be felled. You fell front over back, as you do in the quilt-as-you-go method. If you are felling your seams, it is a good idea to plan ahead and cut body seams with a wider allowance than usual. For example, leave from three-quarters of an inch to an inch (18–25 mm) seam instead of one-half inch (12 mm). You need a little extra fabric to cover the seam bulk.

Do the seam trimming in layers, starting with the batting. Cut it as close to the stitching line as possible, then trim the shell and lining layers. Turn under the seam allowance of the front lining or the front layer, depending on which side you are working, and pin it in place over the seam. Top-stitch this by machine, or finish by hand.

BINDING THE SEAMS

Binding is a method of finishing body seams that can be used for either hand- or machine-quilted garments, and the binding may be flat or fold-over. The binding may also vary in width and color, and you can purchase it ready-made or make your own. An extra yard of fabric of your choice should be plenty for binding body seams as well as outside edges. Whether or not your garment is reversible, the binding will show. Therefore, it will become part of the garment design, and you must think of it in this way and choose the fabric for binding accordingly.

If the body seams are straight, you can cut the binding on the straight grain. Whenever there is a curve involved, you should cut the binding on the bias. Whenever possible, use the binding without piecing; but if you need to piece for length, do it before the binding is applied. Both straight-grain and bias strips are pieced together on straight grain. Since the seams will be covered with binding, you must decide if the binding will be on the shell or lining side, and usually the design of the garment itself will make this decision obvious. You must also decide whether to sew the binding on by hand, machine, or a combination of machine and hand stitching. This last looks better.

The binding should be wide enough to cover the seam comfortably—an inch, or even an inch and a half (3–4 cm) for some garments is plenty. For single-width binding, cut the strips a half-inch (12 mm) wider than the finished size to give you two quarter-inch (6-mm) seam allowances. Press these under carefully and accurately before you start sewing; a wavy, irregular line will spoil the look of the garment. Now, machine stitch the body seams, the sides and shoulders, and any others, including sleeve seams. Trim these seams, finger press them open, and pin the binding in place over them. You can hand sew each edge in place or top-

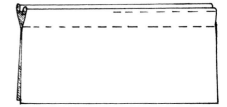

Fig. 37. *A mock French seam for finishing. Batt is trimmed close after first stitching, then the raw edges of the shell and lining are turned in evenly toward each other and stitched again.*

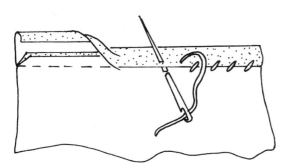

Fig. 38a. *Single bias used to finish seam or outside edge. Bias is machine stitched to garment, then hand finished.*

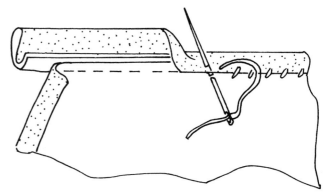

Fig. 38b. *French or double bias, stitched to garment edge. Bias encases seam allowances, and folded edge is caught with hand stitching to garment.*

stitch the edges with machine. Of course, the machine stitching will be visible from the other side, and if you don't want it to show use the hand technique. Ribbon or braid may be substituted for a flat binding, and if you do use either of them, chances are you want it on the outside of the garment where it would show to better advantage.

You can also stitch one edge of your binding, either single or double, in the seam itself, but this means you will be stitching through seven layers. If you do this, press under only one seam allowance of a single binding and leave the other edge flat. Line it up along the seam so that the quarter-inch (6-mm) stitching line of the binding is aligned with the half-inch or five-eighths-inch (12- 15-mm) stitching line of the garment. Pin in place, then stitch through all layers. Trim the garment seams as before, turn the binding over the seam, and finish by hand or machine.

Follow the same procedure if the binding is double. Stitch the two raw edges of the binding into the seam. Instead of a pressed-under seam allowance along the other edge of the binding, you now have a folded edge, and you can hand sew or machine top-stitch this in place.

Double binding is a little stronger than the single, and I think it also has an advantage in ease of application. Refer back to the section on bias strips in Chapter 5, in Developing Design: With Appliqué, and use this method to make the double binding for seams. In other words, if you want the finished width to be one inch (2.5 cm), cut a three-inch (7.5-cm) bias strip, fold it in the middle lengthwise, and stitch the raw edges together a half-inch from the edge. Trim this seam, then work it with your fingers so that it lies in the middle of the strip and not on one edge. You now have a double strip with two folded edges, ready to apply.

STAND-UP OR FOLD-OVER BINDING

With the stand-up or fold-over method, you use the same type of binding as you would for flat binding. The difference is that you stitch one edge of the binding into each seam you want to finish this way—the seven-layer stack again. Then trim the seams *evenly* to half the width of the binding, and keep the seams together, not opened. The binding folds over the raw edges of these seams, and you finish the other edges of the binding by hand, catching it to the seam just stitched so nothing shows. I think it is far easier to use this method with the combination of machine and hand stitching than to try to machine stitch this last step. All of these body seams must be finished before the outside edges are

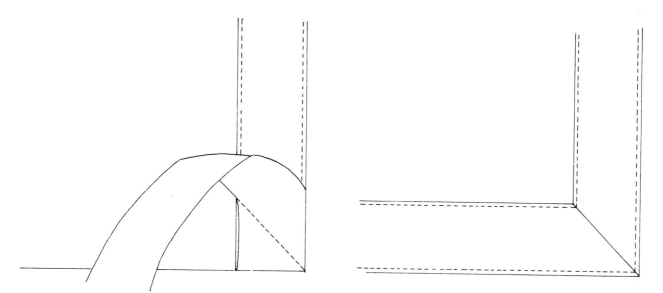

Fig. 39a. *Mitering a corner with ribbon or fabric strips topstitched to outside of garment.*

Fig. 39b. *Finished miter.*

bound or faced, since the raw edges of the bindings and garment will be caught in the final steps.

I'd like to make one last suggestion about stitching quilted seams together. If your fabric is a little heavier than medium weight, or if you've used a thicker batt or two layers of thin matting, you may feel there is just more bulk in the seams than you want to deal with. If so, trim the batting back just enough so that it will not be caught in the seam when it's stitched; the batt will then go up to the seam but not in it, and this eliminates a lot of bulk.

Fig. 40. *Shaping bias strips or ribbon with steam iron to fit curved or shaped surface.*

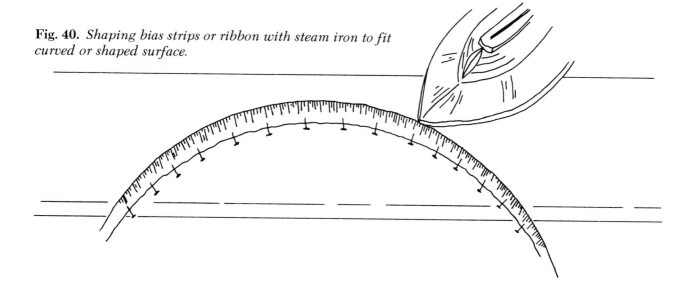

Reversible garments, or garments quilted through both shell and lining fabrics, usually have bound edges. Even the wide front bands of the Tibetan coat or haori coats could almost be called bindings. They are stitched in the same way, but their finished width is much wider.

When you are ready to finish the edges, be sure you have enough binding to cover the distance planned. Wider bands usually go up one side of the front, around the neck, and down the other front, then are incorporated in a separate hem band. A narrower binding often starts at the bottom of a side seam, goes along the hem edge to the front, up the front, around the neck (and/or collar), down the other front, around the bottom, and back to the starting point.

Again, I think you might have better luck with a combination of machine and hand stitching here. Stitch one side of the binding to the edge of the garment by machine, then turn the binding over the raw edges and finish by hand.

Use the same method if your garment has not been quilted through the lining but has a separate lining. Join all seams of the lining together, press, then fit the lining into the garment, matching outside edges and armholes. Pin or baste these edges together, then stitch the binding or band through garment and separate lining, and finish as before.

Like the edges of quilts, the edges of garments are more likely to wear first, and often it is advisable to use the double or French binding around the edges rather than the single fold. The wider bands usually have been quilted or at least have a layer of filler in them, so they are taken care of.

If your garment is to close rather than hang open, you'll have to plan on this before you wrap everything up and call it finis. Buttonholes or frogs of course won't affect the binding; all edges can be finished first. However, if you want to close a garment with ties or loops for buttons, the ties and loops must be made and basted in place along the front edges before the binding is stitched. These ties or loops will be caught in the stitching and will be more secure than if sewed on by hand later—although this certainly can be done. Frogs are attached by hand after the garment is finished.

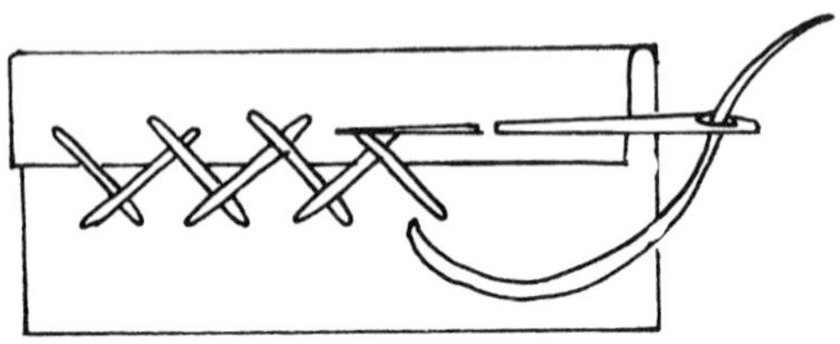

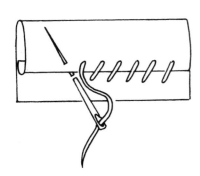

Fig. 41a. *Hem or seam sewed with catch stitch (herringbone).*

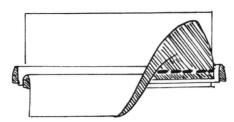

Fig. 42. *Piping (fabric-covered cord) stitched in seam for design accent.*

Fig. 41b. *Hem or seam sewed with overcast or hemming stitch.*

FINISHING A GARMENT WITH A SEAMED EDGE

Finishing a garment with a seamed edge applies to a garment quilted, then "lined to the edge."

All seams in both garment and lining have been stitched and the lining pressed. Put the lining against the garment, right sides together, and pin in place, matching the raw edges. Start stitching at the hem edge of the back section, and stitch all the way around, leaving an opening, usually ten to twelve inches (25–30 cm), to turn the garment to the right side after the seams are trimmed. Sometimes if you plan to add a collar or scarf at the last minute you can stitch all the way around the outside, starting at one neck edge and ending at the other, then turn the garment through the open neck edge.

Once the garment is turned, work the seam with your fingers so that it lies along the edge and doesn't turn or roll to either side. Then, use a line of hand or machine stitching through all layers, close to the seamed edge, to hold it all in shape forever.

When using a separate lining for a jacket or coat, it is better to add sleeves later. Seam the bottom edge of the sleeve to the lining, then pull the lining to the inside of the sleeve. Stitch the sleeve cap to the garment, *keeping the lining free.* Trim the seam, then sew the sleeve lining to the body of the garment at the sleeve seam, using tiny hand stitches.

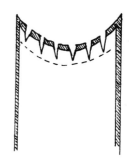

Fig. 44a. *Clipping an inside curved stitched seam for ease in turning.*

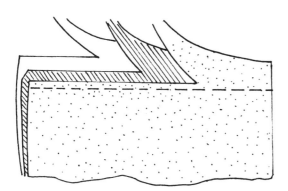

Fig. 43. *Grading a seam after stitching. White area represents shell or outside, striped area represents filler or batt, and dotted area represents lining. Filler and lining can also be trimmed together, close to the stitching line.*

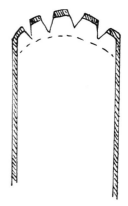

Fig. 44b. *Notching an outside curved stitched seam to get rid of excess fabric.*

There is a last way to join seams of your quilted garment. (I shouldn't say "last," or you might come up with something else behind my back. At any rate, we can call it another way.) It is quite effective used on a panel coat, such as the Tibetan coat or Turkish coat, for then the stitching takes on importance and becomes part of the design. There isn't much point in doing this unless it is going to show.

Cut each panel and panel lining, and for goodness sake be accurate; if you aren't, life may become suddenly unbearable when you get ready to join the panels together. This is also a good time to try quilting a garment without a filler, or, if you don't want to settle for that, use a thin batt such as Fairfield's Cotton Classic, or cotton flannel, or the old-fashioned cotton batt. Put the lining and shell sections together, right sides facing, and stitch all the way around, leaving an opening along one long side large enough to turn the panel. Trim the seam, turn, press, and close the opening by hand, using a blind or slip stitch. Now quilt each panel, then butt the panels together and join them with a decorative stitch on the sewing machine. As you well know, these stitches are built into the machine or are on cams, so that they take advantage of the full swing of the needle. Half of the stitch will be on one side, half on the other, and you will end up with a very effective plus as far as design is concerned.

You may join these sections by hand, if you prefer. Use perle cotton or embroidery floss, and use a herringbone, open chain, or ladder stitch to join the sections.

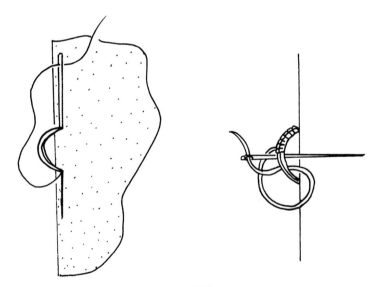

Fig. 45. *Thread loops for small buttons.*

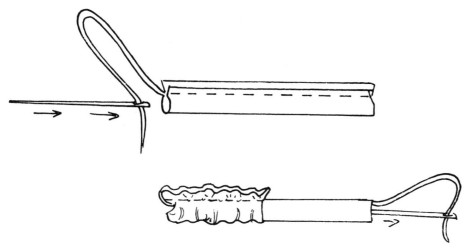

Fig. 46. *Making a bias tube: (a) strip folded and stitched, right sides of fabric inside; (b) turning tube to use for loops, frogs, or trim.*

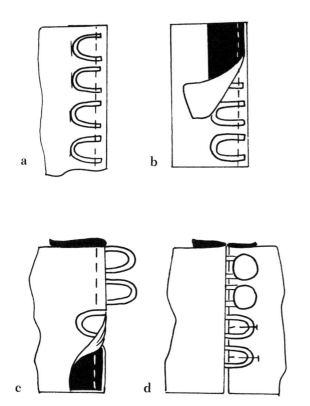

Fig. 47. *Fabric loops of bias tubing used as closures:*
a) measured and basted in place;
b) lining or facing placed over basted loops, right sides together, then stitched;
c) lining or facing turned to inside of garment;
d) finished loops and buttons on front of garment.

CLOSURES

Closures, if you use them, are part of the design of the jacket, and they must be compatible and look like they belong. even if the garment is worn open. Bound buttonholes are difficult to do in quilted fabrics but can be done if they are not too small and you are careful about finishing both sides neatly. A "worked" buttonhole is machine stitched with a zigzag stitch or hand sewn with a buttonhole stitch. They can be put in when a garment is finished.

Ties and button loops may be of purchased ribbon, cord, or braid, or you can make your own bias tubing and use that. Buttons may be real buttons, beads, metal ornaments, fabric-covered balls, or anything else you want to use.

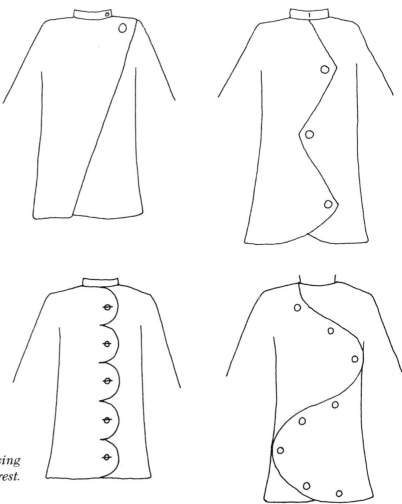

Fig. 48. *Ways to change the front closing of a jacket, vest, or coat to add interest.*

Fig. 49. *Three styles of frogs made from bias tubing.*

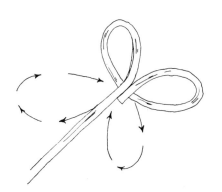

Fig. 50a. *Making loops for simple frog.*

Fig. 50b. *Final looping and securing of frog; stitches underneath.*

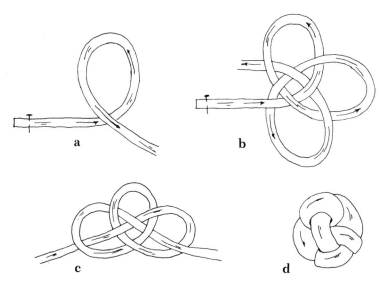

Fig. 51. *Making a Chinese ball button:*
a) first loop of bias tubing or cord;
b) making next two loops;
c) tightening loops to form knotted button;
d) completed button, tacked securely on underside.

Frogs can be purchased or you can make your own. They can be simple or elaborate and any size. If you make your own, you should also make the Chinese ball buttons to go with them.

These closures show, and there are others that won't but that are often necessary—Velcro and silk-covered snaps or hooks come to mind. If these are used for front closings, the garment probably should be worn closed to look its best.

Prairie Points no. 2 and 3 with a buttonhole worked in the point may also be used effectively for closing (see page 79).

11

AFTER-THOUGHTS

Many of you quilters began by making a quilt for yourself, then went on to make a quilt or two for your children or other members of your family and as gifts to treasured friends. After that, many of you began to make quilts to sell. This pattern repeats itself with quilted clothes. Many of you have already been working in this creative and rewarding area, first, perhaps, making a garment for yourself, then for family and friends, and then, perhaps, to sell through a craft show or a gallery.

If there ever were boundary lines between quilters and home sewers as far as clothing is concerned, they've been wiped out. Quilter-turned-sewer and sewer-turned-quilter are equal, each as talented and enthusiastic as the other. Your clothing designs are uniquely expressive; they range from classic and understated to outrageous but are all truly one of a kind.

If—or when—you decide you want to sell your work, then you must direct your efforts to such a venture. Choose garment styles that won't take forever to make, since your time is valuable. You will never get paid for its full worth or for all the time it takes to turn out a professional, stunning outfit, so you want to make every minute count. Set a salary or wage for yourself on an hourly basis, and the next time you make a quilted garment, keep an accurate time check. Also, keep an accurate list of all the materials you use and what you paid for them. Do the best work you can; if something isn't right, do it over. Any customer willing to pay the price for a piece of art work is entitled to the best possible product.

Know your market, and know how to reach it. If you want to specialize in a certain type of garment, then do some market research. Visit local galleries and shops or boutique areas in department stores. Visit craft fairs and talk to other craftsmen. If you don't want to or can't produce in quantity but prefer one-of-a-kind, or even two- or three-of-a-kind garments, then make up a dozen garments and try to arrange for a local shop to sponsor you in an exhibit and sale. Shops and galleries usually take 40 percent of the purchase price as their commission, and if your work is exceptional it would be worth a gamble for them. They also might buy outright; if so, their markup would be at least double the price they pay you.

You might rent space at a craft show and try selling the clothes yourself. Be sure you have sufficient stock on hand, be prepared to keep books or accounts, and have a space with a mirror to use as a little fitting room.

All of this depends on what you want to do and whether you have time to devote to it. If your home life is too involved at the moment, then you may have to use your own personal time to make quilted clothes and use them as therapy, solace, and salvation from the rigors of routine, for they are all of these things.

If the garments you make are to be washed, be sure everything you use in or on the garment is also washable. Preshrink to be on the safe side—you will also be ensuring that fabrics (especially the dark ones) won't bleed with excess dye. If you sell or give your garment away, add a hangtag with care instructions. Nearly everything I make is to be dry cleaned only, for I use a mixture of fabrics, and I am not sure about the washability of some; also, many embellishments don't take kindly to a bath. Occasionally I make what I call a purely practical garment, a jacket or vest to wear day after day, its purpose being solely to keep me warm. For these garments, I do prewash fabrics, for I like to toss the "purely practicals" into the washing machine without having nightmares.

Some cleaners shy away from beads and sequins and other decorations. If you can, sew these first to net or organza and then appliqué or tack them in place on the garment so that they can be removed before cleaning. I take my chances on almost everything and so far have had no trouble, but I do caution cleaners about sequins, which sometimes melt if they get near heat.

All the techniques and ideas I've written about in this book have worked for me, and I want to pass them on to you. I've tried to include everything, but it is very possible I've left out some points—points that *you* know about and help you in your work. There are many ways to do things, and I'm quite sure you've found some that may be new to me. How I wish I could get together for a good rap session and exchange some more ideas!

Work—any kind of work—does not always go full steam ahead. I've hit dead-ends many a time. My work grinds to a halt and so do I. Nothing seems to go right. Sometimes I wonder if I'm crazy, why on earth I'm knocking myself out to do things that aren't turning out well at all, and I think maybe I should quit all this nonsense and try something sensible for a change. Thank heavens I don't have these attacks often, but when one comes I get up and walk away from it. I try not to push or shove; leaving it is better. I take a walk, read a book, watch TV, make some fudge, bake some bread, or go to a museum. I often go to New York, for a day in that wonderful marvelous madhouse is pure therapy for me, and I come home refreshed and ready to go again.

My work and play are so intertwined I hardly know where one ends and the other begins. I go from typewriter to sewing machine to hand work to piano with what I like to think is a well-developed rhythm, like a runner who is training for a marathon and is continually getting a second wind. For more than twenty-five years, I've played piano for eight men in a Dixieland jazz band. All of these men have other jobs (which pay the mortgages, buy the groceries, and pay school tuitions), but they love the music as much as I do. Music parallels all art and craft, for it is pure creation too, especially jazz and blues. Both are based on melodies, usually simple eight- or twelve-bar tunes, but after that—look out! Each musician is free to improvise, give his own interpretation of what he sees in the music, what he feels, what he hears. What the rest of us hear is pure invention, innovation, a combination of notes and rhythms that belong to the soloist alone and that no one else can duplicate.

We are soloists in fabric work too. Our base may not be a simple melody, but it is often a simple design, or an idea, and then we are free to improvise on our theme and create our own melodic interpretation. When we sew and quilt a garment, whether by hand or machine or a happy mix of the two, we are writing our own songs. And now, the "great garment" is at hand—your hand.

12

WHAT THEY SAY, AND HOW THEY WORK AND FEEL

Both the color and the black-and-white photographs in this book have shown you the diversity of the original and unique work that many different fiber artists, quilters, and home sewers have turned out. They work on many different levels, but they all have one thing in common: they want to express themselves as creatively as possible in the field of wearable art. All of the clothes pictured here are quilted, for quilting undeniably adds a dimension of depth and texture impossible to achieve in any other way.

A few of these people have written me in detail about their attitudes and approach to their work and the techniques they use in both design and construction. I am passing these "statements" on to you. I do not have quotes from all whose work is represented here, but all are certainly included. Each of them has a responsibility and a dedication toward this work, and, in this way, one person can speak for many.

Betty Mason. A California designer and quilter, Betty is also the author of *Betty's Basic Boxes*. Her real work and love, she says, is designing, writing, and sewing, whether it concerns clothes, dolls, or boxes, none of which is work, but fun and love. She adds: "Unfortunately, the landlord does not accept dolls, clothes, or boxes in exchange for rent, so I fill out the petty cash department by working three days a week as a paralegal assistant." Betty's landlord is a silly man indeed.

Janet Higgins. Janet is from Tennessee and loves rich, sumptuous fabrics, such as satins, silks, and metallics. She is drawn to the wonderful reflective quality of the materials and the way light plays off surfaces. Janet says she has a romantic nature and baroque sensibility, and she feels, definitely, that more is better than less. She loves lots of color, lots of decoration, and although the clothes she creates are theatrical, she uses hard-edge geometric shapes to keep them from getting out of hand. She hopes the wearer will "escape" into her clothes. She loves making beautiful clothes for people to wear. The clothes are functional, but she also believes the world needs more color, more flash, and more energy, which can be provided in wearable art.

Janet's art evolved gradually from two conflicting interests—kinetics and flat pattern. Originally she created costumes for theater and dance, and she works in strong colors, usually solid shades, sparked by laces, sequins, and ribbons. She designs her quilting pattern on paper, bastes it to the batting, then quilts through the paper from the wrong side of the garment. She uses heavy silk buttonhole twist wound on the bobbin, then machine quilts with regular thread in the needle assembly; the heavy quilting, of course, shows on the outside of the garment.

Lesly-Claire Greenberg. Lesly-Claire of Virginia designs and markets her patterns under the Quilt Arts label. She concentrates on garments rather than wall quilts and says they are divided into two groups—exhibition work and street wear. Sometimes these are interchangeable, but usually the street wear clothes are more disciplined and perhaps have wider appeal. She starts projects with a small sketch and goes on from there, preferring to do most of her work directly with fabric. She says she often goes to bed with dishes in the sink and housework literally sandwiched in during odd times over the weekends—and she wouldn't have it any other way.

Jo Ann Giordano. An Indiana fiber artist, Jo Ann uses color and pattern as the focus of her work. She uses silk screen printing to explore spatial effects with color, to create repeated images, and to work with the juxtaposition of different patterns. She is influenced by Oriental art and costume and in her fabric printing has used geometric patterns as well as images from scientific photographs. Quilting enhances the printed patterns and adds a rich tactile quality. Jo Ann used an image of atomic particle tracks with superimposed geometric pattern for the Chinese vest and printed on cotton sateen. For the "Samurai" vest, a "ritual" piece, she printed fabric with images from oscilloscope wave patterns, then pieced it using acetate, rayon, and resist-dyed cottons for the total effect. The resist-dyed fabric was done in the traditional Japanese manner of wrapping the fabric around a pole and binding and compressing it before dyeing. This process is called *boumaki.*

Leslie English. A New York artist, Leslie sees life as continual invention with new relationships of form and color. She creates her clothing in a spirit of play and excitement and as the result of thought exploration. She feels her costumes may be viewed two-dimensionally, like paintings; the designs from front and back flow into each other as they do from outside to inside. Linings are often more ornate than the outside shell, but above all the clothes must feel good to the wearer. She uses silk, velvet, wool, and cotton in her work, with a filler of woven or unspun lambswool. She derives many of her ideas from Middle Eastern traditional costumes but gives a contemporary effect to them. Almost all of her garments are quilted to create surface interest and a sculptural element.

Carol Ward. An Indiana artist, Carol enjoys the challenge and mystery (she calls it magic) of combining elements, especially unrelated elements, to make a cohesive whole. She considers wearable art an extension of other art forms and finds no conflict between art forms that are functional and those that are simply decorative. Any art form, Carol says, should have that uniqueness and wonder that makes it enjoyable and appreciated at any level.

Marilyn Price. An Indiana fiber artist, Marilyn excels in silk screening fabric and uses this technique for many of the unique garments she creates. She also silk screens the designs on her quilts, many of which have been prize winners. Recently she was chosen to work with Miriam Schapiro, a well-known New York artist, to create a seven-foot square quilt. Miriam designed the quilt, and Marilyn silk screened the design. They then found five quilters to help appliqué and quilt. The finished quilt was a collaboration between two artistic groups—painters and quilters. Quilting added both depth and texture to the design, and the quilt is now part of a traveling exhibit emphasizing women in the arts.

Marilyn and Carol Ward organized the first wearable art show for the Indianapolis Museum of Art, which featured only Indiana artists. Their garments are sold in boutiques and galleries, and their work is steadily in demand.

Joy Stocksdale. A designer and fiber artist from California, Joy enjoys creating innovative clothing. She says she is influenced by Charles Mackintosh and art nouveau. Like Janet Higgins and others, she quilts from the lining side, using heavy thread in the bobbin, and stitches through tracing paper with the design drawn on it. The use of paper also keeps the work from puckering. Joy did all the quilting for the velveteen coat, *then* painted it, using a stiff brush. Her shadow-quilted garments have a muted, misty effect, created by organza layering over felt.

Judy Mathieson. A creative, prolific quiltmaker and designer from California, Judy is also a quilting teacher. She has developed and marketed patterns for clothes as well. She used flannel as a filler in her mola jacket and used "a marvelous ethnic-looking border print on sleeves and cuffs and down the front." She added shi-sha mirrors over the flowers.

Marjorie Puckett. A California designer known primarily for her book *String Quilts 'N Things*, a how-to textbook on string patchwork, Marjorie's thrust is toward clothing rather than quilts. She also designs for Simplicity Patterns, turning out six patterns a year for them. The patterns she designs can easily be varied so that no two garments look alike, although her emphasis is on string piecing. Fabric created with this technique can also be used for appliqués.

Dorothy Lazara. Dorothy is from New York and often adds soft-sculpture work to her garments as added interest and dimension. She uses trapunto, machine quilting, machine embroidery, and both machine and hand appliqué in her work. Some sections are separately constructed, stuffed, and then sewed in place. Dorothy's garments are designed to be whimsical; the themes she uses in her work (such as Chinese art) satirize the importance of traditional art forms.

GLOSSARY OF BRITISH EQUIVALENTS FOR AMERICAN TERMS

American Term	British Equivalent
All-cotton sheet-blankets	Winceyette sheets
Architect's triangle	Set square
Batt/batting	Padding or wadding
Braid	Plait
Compass	Pair of compasses
False quilting	Flat quilting
Flannel	Winceyette
Floss	Thread
Muslin	(Unbleached) calico
A muslin	A toile
Pellon	Vilene
Polyfil	A soft filling of the kind used to stuff toys
Sashing	Lattice strips
Woof	Weft

BIBLIOGRAPHY

AVERY, VIRGINIA. *The Big Book of Appliqué.* New York, Scribners, 1978 (London, Bell & Hyman).

BRADKIN, CHERYL GREIDER. *The Seminole Patchwork Book.* Published by the author, 1978.

BROWN, ELSA. *Creative Quilting.* New York, Watson Guptill, 1975.

LANE, MAGGIE. *Oriental Patchwork.* New York, Scribners, 1978 (London, Bell & Hyman).

MORGAN, MARY, and MOSTELLER, DEE. *Trapunto and Other Forms of Raised Quilting.* New York, Scribners, 1977.

PORCELLA, YVONNE. *Pieced Clothing.* Modesto, California, Porcella Studios, 1980.

PUCKETT, MARJORIE. *String Quilts 'N Things.* Santa Ana, California, Orange Patchwork, 1979.

WIECHEC, PHILOMENA. *Celtic Quilt Designs.* Saratoga, California, Celtic Design Co.

UNITED KINGDOM SUPPLIERS

John Lewis & Co. Ltd
Oxford Street
London W1A 1EX
Tel. 01-629 7711

McCullock & Wallis Ltd
25-26 Dering Street
London W1R OBH
Tel. 01-629 0311

Needle Needs Ltd
20 Beauchamp Place
London SW3
Tel. 01-589 2361

*The Patchwork Dog & The Calico Cat
21 Chalk Farm Road
London NW1
Tel. 01-485 1239

*The Quiltery
Tacolneston
Norwich
Norfolk NR16 1DW

*The Silver Thimble
33 Gay Street
Bath
Avon BA1 2NT

*The Stables Studio
Dene Lane
Aston
Nr. Stevenage
Herts SG2 7EP
Tel. 0438- 88271

*Strawberry Fayre Fabrics
P.O. Box 95
Cheltenham
Gloucestershire GL53 9RQ

*Mail order available.

INDEX